Internet of Things with Arduino and Bolt

By
Ashwin Pajankar

BPB PUBLICATIONS

ii

FIRST EDITION 2018

Copyright © BPB Publications, INDIA

ISBN: 978-93-8728-426-5

LIMITS OF LIABILITY AND DISCLAIMER OF WARRANTY

Distributors:

BPB PUBLICATIONS
20, Ansari Road, Darya Ganj
New Delhi-110002
Ph: 23254990/23254991

BPB BOOK CENTRE
376 Old Lajpat Rai Market,
Delhi-110006
Ph: 23861747

DECCAN AGENCIES
4-3-329, Bank Street,
Hyderabad-500195
Ph: 24756967/24756400

MICRO MEDIA
Shop No. 5, Mahendra Chambers, 150
DN Rd. Next to Capital Cinema, V.T.
(C.S.T.) Station, MUMBAI-400 001
Ph: 22078296/22078297

Published by Manish Jain for BPB Publications, 20, Ansari Road, Darya Ganj, New Delhi-110002 and Printed at Repro India Limited, New Delhi

PREFACE

The author is confident that the present work in form of this book will come as a relief to the students, makers, and professionals alike wishing to go through a comprehensive work explaining difficult concepts related to Arduino platform, the Arduino ecosystem, and IoT in the layman's language. The book offers a variety of practical IoT projects with electronic components and sensors. Also this is the one of the very first printed books on the Arduino platform which offers detailed instructions on setup of Arduino Tian Board.

This book promises to be a very good starting point for complete novice learners and is quiet an asset to advanced readers too. The author has written the book so that the beginners will learn the concepts related to Arduino ecosystem and IoT in a step-by-step approach.

Though this book is not written according to syllabus of any University, students pursuing science and engineering degrees (B.E./B.Tech/B.Sc./M.E./M.Tech./M.Sc.) in Computer Science, Electronics, Instru- mentation, Telecommunications, and Electrical streams will find this book immensely beneficial and helpful for their projects and practical work. Software and Information Technology Professionals who begins to learn microcontrollers or want to switch their careers to IoT (Internet of Things) will also benefit from this book.

It is said "To err is human, to forgive divine". In this light the author wishes that the shortcomings of the book will be forgiven. At the same time, the author is open to any kind of constructive criticisms, feedback, corrections, and sugges- tions for further improvement. All intelligent suggestions are welcome and author will try his best to incorporate such in valuable suggestions in the subse- quent editions of this book.

Acknowledgement

No task is a single man's effort. Cooperation and Coordination of various peoples at different levels go into successful implementation of this book.

There is always a sense of gratitude, which everyone expresses to the others for the help they render during difficult phases of life and to achieve the goal already set. It is impossible to thank individually but I am hereby making a humble effort to thank and acknowledge some of them.

I would like to thank Mr. Manish Jain for giving me an opportunity to write for BPB Publications. Writing for BPB has been my dream for me for last 15 years as I grew up reading books authored by Yashwant Kanetkar. I have published more than 10 books till now and this is my second book for BPB.

I would like to thank Mr. Pranav Pai Vernekar (Co-Founder and CEO at Inventrom- Bolt IoT) for helping me with essential hardware components for a couple of chapters in the book. I would also like to thank his team for helping me to build projects with Bolt platform.

Finally, I want to thank everyone who has directly or indirectly contributed to complete this authentic piece of work.

Table of Contents

Chapter 1

Basics of Internet of Things

We are going to start our exciting journey in the world of Internet of Things. This is the very first chapter of this book and I will cover the essence of the concepts related to Internet of Things. The chapter covers theoretical explanations of the concepts required to go ahead.

I have deliberately kept the chapter short, precise, and simple to make the concepts easily comprehensible to the beginners. There is also a list of URLs in the end of chapter, which readers can visit to gain more in-depth understanding of the concepts related to Internet of Things.

What is Internet of Things?

Internet of Things (abbreviated as IoT) has always been present since the era of computing in some form or the other. However, due to the recent technological advances, we are able to experience it more readily than earlier. So, let us first see what IoT is.

IoT is a network of real-life objects (such as physical devices, vehicles, and home appliances) embedded with electronic sensors, related software programs, and network/Internet connectivity, which enables these objects to connect to each other and send, receive, and store data.

This is the simplest definition of IoT. IoT allows the state real-life objects to be sensed and/or controlled remotely across the existing networks and Internet infrastructure. It results in more direct integration of the physical world into cyberworld. For us (humans), it means less manual intervention and more automation of day-to-day activities.

Before going forward, let us consider a simple real-life example of an IoT-based system that results in reduced human intervention. Let's say Bob is a farmer who lives 8 miles (5 kilometers) away from his farm. There is a source of water in his farm (well or small lake), which is used to water his crops. There is an electric pump near the source of water, which draws the water from the source and releases it into irrigation system of his farms. The crops that Bob plants need a regular supply of water and must be watered twice daily at the interval of 12 hours. The first stage of automation would be to create a small circuit with a microprocessor/microcontroller, a clock, and relay to regularly turn the pump on and off. However, Bob has no way to know whether the system is working properly when he is away. Also, if Bob changes the crop, the system has to be reset and the interval at which the pump operates has to be changed. Bob has to call the technician every season to change the settings of this automation.

However, if we connect the microprocessor/microcontroller connected to the pump to the Internet and develop a small mobile application that allows Bob to see and change the status of pump at his convenience, it will really be a great solution. The mobile-based application can also have settings for periodic operation of pump, which could be easily altered by users such as Bob. Also, sending a text message (SMS) or a WhatsApp message to Bob when the task of water pumping is done will be a great additon. We can also have provision of automatically notifying the maintenance technician in case of trouble with the pump. This is one of the simplest and real-life implementation of IoT. This is no way a case that truly exploits the power of devices and unprecedented level of connectivity we enjoy today. However, we are just getting started with IoT. Throughout this book, we will study in detail the technologies that enable IoT and many such examples.

Beginning of IoT

As aforementioned in the previous section, IoT existed since the dawn of computer-based automation and networking. It was just not addressed with the term IoT. The root of the term IoT could be traced back to the **Auto-ID Center at the Massachusetts Institute of Technology (MIT)**. The Auto-ID Center was founded in the year 1999, and initially, it worked on networked **radio-frequency identification (RFID)** technology. The term IoT was coined by Kevin Ashton when he was working with **Proctor and Gamble**. He contributed in establishing the Auto-ID Center at MIT. Since then, the IoT and the ecosystem have evolved tremendously. Apart from the RFID, IoT uses various technologies, such as **near-field communications(NFC)**, barcodes, and QRcodes for identifying the things. Many organizations have commercialized the concept and launchedvarious IoT-enabled products in the market.
In the earlier days of development and maturity, the usage of the term IoT was not as widespread and popular as it is today. In the last two decades, the technology industry went through a profound transformation. This is the major factor in the rapid spread of Internet-based services and devices throughout the globe. The following factors have influenced the growth of IoT industry.

Advances in the semiconductor technology

According to the **Moore's law**, the number of transistors in an **integrated circuit (IC)** doubles every two years. A decade ago, ICs were fabricated with 45 nanometer process. As of writing of this book, the industry is already moving toward 7 nanometer process. As a result, the microprocessors and microcontrollers are packed with more computing power than earlier. Microprocessors and microcontrollers are essential in an IoT ecosystem as they provide all the computation, communication, and control capabilities for any IoT-based system. More computing power directly translates into faster processing of data and faster communication.

Rise of single-board computers and microcontroller-based boards

The last five years have witnessed unprecedented boom in **single-board computers (SBCs)** such as Raspberry Pi and Banana Pro, as well as microcontroller-based development platforms such as Arduino. Small in size, SBCs and microcontroller boards are inspiring many young and innovative minds. This era is comparable to mid-1980s when **Commodore 64** and **Commodore 128** inspired an entire generation to learn programming and fueled the rise of Silicon Valley of USA.

Internet availability

Well until earlier in this century, an Internet connection meant the dial-up connection over the telephone line for most of the consumers. However, with the rise of mobile telephony, Internet, and hence, connectivity is not an issue anymore. A large portion of Internet consumers are using various methods such asdial-up, broadband, cable connection, 3G, and 4G LTE for accessing the Internet.

Advances in wireless technologies

Besides Wi-Fi, various new technologies suchas NFC, RFID, and Bluetooth have enabled the mobile devices to form ad-hoc networks and exchange data with one another. The IoT ecosystem is enriched by the presence of these technologies and creatively uses these methods of communications between mobile devices.

Ubiquity of affordable mobile devices

Today, one can purchase an Android OS phone with Wi-Fi, 4G LTE, and Bluetooth for as little as 80 US dollars. IoT-based systems can integrate with existing mobile devices, networks, and services to connect to the Internet to exchange data and interact with the real world.

Because of the aforementioned enabling factors, we are witnessing a boom in IoT-based products, services, and solutions in the market.

Applications of IoT

IoT has immense applications in various areas. There is a very good chance that the readers of this book are themselves using one of the IoT-enabled products or services. Let's have a look at a few areas where IoT is used.

Consumer products

IoT can be seamlessly integrated into day-to-day consumer products such as refrigerators, televisions, and other home appliances. Smart and connected devices are good examples. If you are a fitness enthusiast, then personal devices such as smart watch and smart health monitor are the best fit for you.

Home automation

Home automation is also known as smart home. It is not a recent concept. Plenty of smart home prototypes and actual products are available since mid-2000s. Having said that, recent developments in IoT and related technologies have prompted many organizations to launch products in home automation. Sometimes, the smart home system integrates various IoT-enabled consumer products to form a local grid and offers a unique and productive end-user experience.

Infrastructure management

IoT-enabled monitoring and remote-controlled systems are extensively used in management of modern infrastructure facilities such as bridges, military installations, server rooms, data centers, and factories. Earlier, when networking technologies were immature, there were dedicated people on the critical sites for monitoring the overall situation. Since the advent of IoT, the human workforce required for monitoring has largely been replaced with advanced sensor networks that monitor the vital parameters at the critical sites and send the messages to the maintenance teams using the Internet.

Manufacturing

State-of-the-art IoT solutions can be used to monitor and remotely operate the production lines in the factories. Most of the automobile manufacturing assembly lines are already mostly automated and can easily be integrated with the Internet for remote operations. Nowadays,only a handful of niche skills, such as engine assembly, require humans for operation in automobile. Also, in the chemical manufacturing processes, it is safer to use automation with IoT for monitoring, as well as production of hazardous chemical products.

Agriculture

In the beginning, we have already discussed a small case study where the farmer Bob needs to water his plants using his mobile phone. We can extend this to agriculture and animal husbandry in general. IoT-enabled services can be used to automate tasks such as watering and monitoring growth of the plants. Already existing automations in majority of the farms in the western hemisphere can be easily extended with IoT by connecting them to the Internet.

Mining

Mining is a hazardous sector where people have to work deep underground. The mining industry already uses many networked and IoT-enabled solutions for tasks such as exploring new areas for resources, checking caves for dangerous gases, and warning about the structural integrity of the mines to the miners.

Healthcare

Healthcare is one of the areas thathave a direct impact on human lives. IoT is actively used in the healthcare monitoring and notification systems. Many research groups in the world are working for creating wearable IoT solutions for healthcare. These IoT solutions and services for healthcare professionals come handy to the caregivers of old, sick, and infirm people.

Environment

Environment is another application of IoT that directly affects lives on a larger scale. With the help of IoT-enabled weather reporting system consisting of sensor networks and mobile-based apps, we can warn people before hand about the impending natural disasters such as volcano eruptions, floods, hurricanes, and earthquakes, thereby minimizing loss of life and property damages.

Transportation

IoT can be integrated into existing transportation system and has far-reaching implications in the areas of smart vehicles, intra-vehicular communication, and smart transportation grid. It can also be used for automated toll collection and smart traffic management.

Advantages of IoT

We are now familiarized with the basics of IoT.Let's discuss the advantages of IoT-enabled solutions and products in brief.

Improved cyber real-world interaction

It is the very first time in the history of technology that real things and objects are represented in the cyberworld. It is estimated that there are multiple times more Internet-connected objects and devices in the world than humans. This allows to form ad-hoc networks and exchange useful information between devices easily.

Automation and reduced human intervention

As the IoT devices continue to be available at an affordable cost widely to general public, more systems and infrastructure facilities have been automated and integrated into the Internet for communications. This has reduced the need for human presence for monitoring. Also, the progress in AI research means the devices can now be smart and are capable of ad-hoc decisions. This also drastically reduces the need for human intervention, if not eliminating it altogether.

Reduced cost and new employment opportunities

As we have seen in the preceding paragraph, monitoring tasks are almost automated with IoT, and it reduces the human presence. This directly translates to economic benefits. It also creates new employment opportunities. People with skills in diverse areas such as computer programming, electronics, and networking have found a new career in the IoT industry.

Challenges associated with IoT

We have seen the advantages of IoT and how it enhances our lives. However, we must not forget, similar toany other technology, IoT comes with its own share of problems. Let us have a brief look at the important challenges posed by IoT.

Security

An IoT service or product is basically a mini computer connected to the Internet. It naturally inherits all the vulnerabilities shared by its bigger cousins. However, knowing that it is connected to your refrigerator makes it truly worrisome. I guess you have gotten the point I am trying to communicate. Security is an active threat that may come in the form of hacking and modifying the source code of the IoT device to make it behave in unintended way.

Privacy

Security is an active risk, whereas privacy is a passive risk. IoT-enabled products and services are tasked with gathering the real-world data ranging from your blood pressure to the vapor pressure in an industrial tank. If that data is exchanged by IoT devices over unsecure networks, the users of such systems are potentially exposing themselves to the theft of personal and financial information thatis sensitive in nature.

Compatibility of protocols

With numerous IoT-enabled devices and frameworks in the market, the compatibility of communications protocols and technologies is a challenge for IoT developers. IoT is still in its infancy, and the technology for communication is getting better over the time. There are several organizations that are developing protocols and standards for IoT devices.

References

- MIT Auto-ID homepage: https://autoidlabs.org/
- Wikipedia page for IoT: https://en.wikipedia.org/wiki/Internet_of_things
- IoT tutorial at Tutorials Point: https://www.tutorialspoint.com/internet_of_
                                    things/index.htm

Summary

In this chapter, we familiarized ourselves with the basic concepts in IoT. This was a very short and concise chapter. From the next chapter, we will get started with the Arduino ecosystem. The next chapter is an informative chapter to get all the readers started with Arduino.

Exercise

- Visit all the links mentioned in the References section to read more aboutIoT.
- Search the Internet for various IoT products and services.

Chapter 2

Introduction to the Arduino Platform

I hope that all of you have gone through the preface and Chapter 1, Basics of Internet of Things. If not, I would recommend you to read them thoroughly. With this chapter, we are starting our journey into the wonderful and amazing world of Arduino platform.

Arduino is an open source electronics prototyping platform and ecosystem. It is based on an easy-to-use hardware and software environment. It is intended for students, artists, designers, hobbyists, enthusiasts, and anyone interested in creating interactive objects or environments.

In this chapter, we will learn the following concepts:
• Microcontrollers
• AVR microcontrollers
• Features of Arduino
• Arduino boards and ecosystem

Microcontrollers

Before we get started with Arduino, we need to understand what a microcontroller is. This is because, basically Arduino is a microcontroller platform. A microcontroller is a small computer on a single integrated circuit (IC). It is a complete package with a microprocessor, onboard memory, and programmable input/output peripherals. Microcontrollers are heavily used in embedded applications.

AVR microcontrollers

AVR is a family of microcontrollers developed by Atmel Corporation. Atmel is America-based designer and manufacturer of microcontrollers. Atmel began the development of AVR microcontrollers in the beginning in 1996. AVR microcontrollers are modified Harvard architecture 8-bit reduced instruction set computer(RISC) single-chip microcontrollers.

A special feature of the AVR family is that it is one of the first families of microcontrollers that have on-chip flash memory. Other competing microcontroller families at that time (late 1990s) had ROM, EPROM, or EEPROM for the program and firmware storage.

The reason we discussed AVR microcontrollers is that Arduino products prominently use various AVR microcontrollers.

You can find more information about AVR on http://www.atmel.com/products/microcontrollers/avr/.

Other microcontrollers and processors used by Arduino boards

In addition to AVR microcontrollers, a couple of development boards from Arduino family (namely, Arduino Zero and MKR1000) use ARM microcontroller units. ARM is another family of RISC microprocessors designed and manufactured by ARM.

Few high-end Arduino boards support Linux, and they have Qualcomm Atheros microprocessors. Examples are Aruino Yun, Arduino Tian, and Arduino Industrial 101. Arduino 101 uses Intel Curie.

In this chapter, we will get familiarized to various Arduino boards and the entire ecosystem in detail.

Who can learn Arduino

The real power of the Arduino platform lies in the fact that it is for everyone. Yes! That might sound like an exaggeration. However, it is truly meant for everyone.

Arduino was originally meant for the students. Its purpose was to provide a low-cost and open source platform and ecosystem to the students to learn electronics and programming. With time, the popularity of Arduino grew, and it has pervaded in many areas.

Today, Arduino is prominently used as the most preferred microcontroller platform in education and academic institutions. It is also extensively used in the embedded systems in the areas of industrial production, healthcare, mining, and traffic monitoring. It has also found place in active research in the areas of modeling, simulation, human and computer interface.

As we have seen, it was meant for students in the beginning. However, now it is actively used by electronics makers, enthusiasts, and hobbyists all around the world to make interactive stuff. It is also used by artists. If you are studying computer science or electronics, there is pretty good chance that you have seen one of the Arduino boards in action.

The following image shows my little neighbor working on an Arduino board for her school project:

High school student working with Arduino for her school project

We can find more information on the Arduino platform on its website https://www.arduino.cc.

Features of Arduino

Arduino is the most preferred platform for the makers nowadays because of the following features:

• **Inexpensive:** Arduino is an inexpensive board. It costs less than the contemporary microcontroller trainer platforms. You can even assemble your own Arduino. The Arduino clones cost even lesser than the official Arduino boards.

• **Cross-platform:** The official Arduino IDE is supported on Windows, Linux, and Mac OSX.

• **Open source hardware:** The diagrams of all the Arduino boards are published under Creative Commons License,and they are open source.

• **Open source software:** Arduino can be programmed with the official Arduino IDE and AVR C programming.

Why Arduino

The features of the Arduino platform that appeal to me are the openness (in terms of hardware and software) and low cost. When we compare Arduino to other popular IoT platforms such as the popular single-board computers (Raspberry Pi and Banana Pro), Arduino beats other platforms in terms of openness and price. Arduino boards are widely available in most of the places. That's why; we will use the Arduino platform and its ecosystem to get started with the hands-on with IoT. However, to do that, we need to know the Arduino platform and the ecosystem in detail. This chapter and the next few chapters cover fundamentals of Arduino, a few important electronic components, and Arduino programming.

Arduino boards and ecosystem

Till now, we've learned what a microcontroller is and also learned that most of the major Arduino boards use AVR microcontrollers. A few Arduino boards also use ARM microprocessors. In this section, we will understand what the Arduino ecosystem is and have a look at few major member boards of the Arduino ecosystem.

Arduino has a very vibrant ecosystem with a plethora of products. These boards and products are grouped into various categories. Let's have a look at each category one by one.

Official Arduino boards

Official Arduino boards carry Arduino brand on them. They are directly supported by the official Arduino IDE. They are licensed to bear the Arduino logo on them. Also, they are manufactured by authorized manufacturers.

The authorized manufacturers pay a royalty for each board that contributes toward keeping Arduino brand running. They sell the boards through the worldwide network of authorized distributors; so, in the case of defective boards, the buyers get the replacement and support officially.

Currently, the official manufacturers are:

• SmartProjects in Italy (http://www.arduinosrl.it)

• Sparkfun in USA (https://www.sparkfun.com)

• DogHunter in China (http://www.doghunter.org)

We can find an exhaustive list of the official Arduino boards at https://www.arduino.cc/en/Main/Products.

Let's have a look at few of the most important ones.

Arduino Uno is the best board for those who are just getting started with the Arduino platform for the first time. It is the most documented and widely used board. It uses the ATmega328P microcontroller. The following is an image of an Arduino Uno Rev 3 board:

Arduino Uno Rev 3

Arduino Leonardo is another entry-level board that uses the ATmega32u4 microcontroller. The following is an image of Arduino Leonardo with headers:

Arduino Leonardo with headers

Next board in the line is Arduino 101 which has 32-bit Intel Curie microcontroller. The following is an image of Arduino 101:

Arduino/Genuino 101

Genuino is a trademark owned by Arduino.

The Arduino Esplora is an Arduino Leonardo-based board with integrated sensors and actuators. It uses the ATmega32u4 microcontroller. The following image depicts an Arduino ESPLORA board:

Arduino Esplora

Arduino Micro is the smallest board of the family, used for interactive computing. The Micro is based on the ATmega32U4 microcontroller. It features a built-in USB for connection with a computer.

Arduino Esplora

The next member of Arduino family is Arduino Nano. It is a breadboard-friendly board based on the ATmega328. The following is an image of an Arduino Nano

Arduino Nano

The boards we've seen till now are made for entry-level users. Let's now see a more advanced line of boards with more functionality.

Arduino Mega is based on the ATmega2560 microcontroller. It gives more I/O pins for use. The following is an image of Arduino Mega 2560 Rev 3:

Arduino Mega 2580 Rev 3

Arduino Zero provides 32-bit extension to the platform established by Arduino Uno R3. It uses the ATSAMD21G18 microcontroller.

Arduino Zero

Another board based on the ATSAMD21G18 microcontroller is Arduino M0 PRO:

Arduino M0 PRO

Now it's time to know about few Linux-based boards that are exclusively used for IoT. The first member is Arduino Yún. It features the Atheros AR9331 microprocessor.

Arduino Yún

Arduino Industrial 101 is Arduino Yún designed with a small form factor.

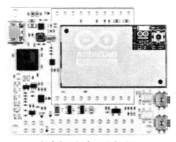

Arduino Industrial 101

Arduino Tian features a more powerful microprocessor Atheros AR9342, which is faster than Atheros 9331

Arduino Tian

Till now, we have seen the Arduino boards that could be used in the projects. Now, we introduce a special category of miniature boards that are used for wearable projects and e-textiles. The first member is Lilypad Arduino USB.

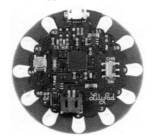

Lilypad Arduino USB

Lilypad Arduino Mainboard uses the ATmega168V or ATmega328V, which are the low-power versions of ATmega168 or ATmega328.

Lilypad Arduino main board

These are the few most prominent original members of the Arduino ecosystem. The complete list can be found at https://www.arduino.cc/en/Main/Products.

Arduino derivatives

Arduino derivatives are licensed derivatives of the official Arduino boards. They are too directly supported by the official Arduino IDE. These products add innovations to the existing designs and cater to a particular subset of users.
The most prominent example is Adafruit Flora.

Adafruit Flora

You can find out more about Flora at https://www.adafruit.com/flora.
Another product is Teensy from PJRC. You can find more details about Teensy at https://www.pjrc.com/teensy/

Teensy by PJRC

Arduino clones

Arduino is an open source hardware, and anyone is free to create his/her own board. Arduino was made open source so that it could be built and tinkered by anyone in the world. The boards that fall under the clone work with the official Arduino IDE and are manufactured by the manufacturers other than official ones. They do not carry the brand name Arduino; however, their names are reflective of their Arduino clone status. Examples include Freeduino and Sainsmart boards.
You can find Freeduino and Sainsmart boardsat https://www.freeduino.org/ and https://www.sainsmart.com/arduino/control-boards/arduino-microcontrollers.html, respectively. There are many similar clones in the market, and most of them are directly compatible with the official Arduino IDE.

Arduino counterfeits

Arduino counterfeitsis a category of Arduino clones and derivatives that bear the Arduino logo and trademark without permission They are detrimental to the entire opensource hardware movement. The real danger of buying the counterfeit Arduino is that, in case of a problem, the manufacturer does not replace the board. Also, coun- terfeit manufacturers do not pay any royalty for using the Arduino brand and logo on their boards. The following link has detailed information about Arduino counterfeits: https://www.arduino.cc/en/Products/Counterfeit

I have not covered Arduino shields in this chapter as I feel that, at this point, the information related to the shields will be a bit overwhelming to the beginners. After we cover the basics in the next few chapters, we will cover the a few Arduino shields in detail.

Assembling your own Arduino Uno board

You can even assemble your own Arduino compatible on a breadboard. This is the true essence of the open source hardware. The recipe can be found at https://ww-w.arduino.cc/en/Main/Standalone.

Where to buy Arduino

We can directly buy Arduino online at https://store.arduino.cc/usa.
If you want to buy from a regional distributor. then visit https://www.arduino.cc/en/-Main/Buy to know the country-wise contacts of the resellers.

Summary

In this chapter, we familiarized ourselves with the Arduino platform and the ecosystem. In the next chapter, we will learn various ways to power an Arduino board and install Arduino IDE on your computer.

Exercise for this chapter

Visit all the links mentioned in the chapter and become familiar with the Arduino ecosystem.

Chapter 3

Getting Started with Arduino

In Chapter 2, Introduction to the Arduino Platform, we learned the basic concepts of microcontroller and AVR microcontroller. We were introduced to the vibrant ecosystem of the Arduino platform for the makers. We understood the advantages of the Arduino platform and the related ecosystem. We also learned from where to purchase Arduino boards.

In this chapter, we will start with some hands-on with Arduino programming with Arduino Uno. We will start studying the basics of Arduino programming in detail from the next chapter. Before we start programming, it is essential to get started with the basics of setting up the environment for Arduino programming at this stage so that, from the next chapter, we can directly study the code examples.

For this chapter, we will need the following hardware components:
- A Windows PC with an Internet connection.
- An Arduino Uno microcontroller or a compatible clone.
- A USB male A to male B cable.
- A DC power supply for Arduino.
- 9V DC battery, 9V battery connector, and 2.1 mm DC barrel jack adapter (male).
- A USB power supply

Let's have a look at each component in detail.

Arduino Uno

We are going to get started with Arduino Uno (or a compatible clone) for our first experience with the Arduino platform.
Let's have a look at the Uno. A Uno or a compatible clone looks like the following:

Arduino Uno

Before we proceed, let's study the technical specifications and detailed descriptions of the pins on the Arduino Uno board.

Technical specifications Arduino Uno Rev 3

Arduino Uno is based on the ATmega328P microcontroller.

 You can find the detailed datasheet of the microcontroller at http://www.atmel.com/Images/Atmel-42735-8-bit-AVR-Microcontroller-ATmega328-328P_Datasheet.pdf

It has 32 KB of flash memory, 0.5 KB of which is used by a bootloader. A bootloader is a small program that runs everytime when the microcontroller is powered or reset. It basically tells the microcontroller what to do next when it is powered on. It is kind of primitive operating system (OS) for the microcontroller. The bootloader comes pre-loaded on the flash memory of the ATmega328P microcontroller installed on Arduino Uno. The detailed discussion about the bootloader is out of the scope for the book. However, interested readers can read and learn more to try different options with the bootloader from the following links:

• https://www.arduino.cc/en/Hacking/Bootloader
• https://www.arduino.cc/en/Hacking/MiniBootloader

Arduino Uno has 2 KB of static RAM (SRAM) and 1 KB of EEPROM.The clock speed of ATmega328P is 16 MHz. The weight of the official Arduino Uno R3 board is 25 grams.

Pin description of Arduino Uno Rev 3

Refer to the following image for the pin numbering and classification:

Arduino pin description diagram

Let's discuss the pins of the Arduino Uno board in detail. In the preceding image, the pins are grouped and labeled. Let's begin from the bottom left.

The bottom left pin is not connected to anything and is used as a placeholder.

The IOREF pin is for providing the logic reference voltage. It is connected to the 5 volt bus.

The RESET pin is used to reset the microcontroller by bringing it low.

Let's have a look at the power pins.

The 3.3V pinprovides the regulated power of 3.3V. The maximum current draw is 50 mA.

The 5V pin supplies regulated power of 5V.

The GND pins are the ground pins.

The Vin pin acts as an external input pin for externally regulated 9–12V power supply for the entire board. If the board is powered by the power jack or USB, this pin is used for 5V output.

Let's see the analog input pins of Arduino Uno. These are located in the bottom right corner in the preceding image. There are six analog pins A0 through A5,and they are used to read the signals from the analog sensors. Each of these pins has a 10-bit resolution. They can work with 1024 (2^10) different values (voltage levels).

There are 14 digital I/O pins on the Arduino Uno board. They can be used for digital input and digital output based on the mode. They are numbered 0 through 13. These operate at 5V and can provide or receive 20mA current. If the current received or pulled exceeds 40 mA for any of these pins, it can permanently damage the board. In addition to the digital I/O function, pins 3, 5, 6, 9, 10, and 11 are used for the 8-bit pulse-width modulation (PWM) output.

Of all the digital I/O pins, several pins have specialized functions.

• **Serial communication:** Pins 0 (RX) and 1 (TX) are used from serial communication.

• **External interrupts:** Pins 2 and 3 are used for configuring to trigger an external interrupt on low value, a rising or falling edge, or a change in value.

• **Serial peripheral interface:** Pins 10 (SS), 11 (MOSI), 12 (MISO), and 13 (SCK) support SPI communication using the SPI library.

• **LED:** Pin 13 has a built-in LED attached to it. When the pin is high, it is ON; when pin is low, it is OFF.

• **Two-wire interface:** Analog pins A4 (SDA) and A5 (SLC) are used for TWI communi-cation using the wire library.

• **Reference Voltage:** The AREF pin is used to set the reference voltage for the analog input pins A0 to A5.

 It would be really interesting to understand the pin mapping between Arduino

Uno board and ATmega328 microcontroller at the URL https://www.ardui-no.cc/en/Hacking/PinMapping168.

How to power Arduino Uno

In this section, we will discuss various ways to power up the Arduino Uno board in detail.

Positions of USB and DC power ports

USB power

We can supply 5V power through the USB port. For that, we need a USB power supply. A USB port of a PC serves the purpose. When connected to a PC with this port for uploading the program, we do not need to use any other power supply. The following image shows a USB A to B cable. Usually, the board is supplied with a cable.

USB A to B

We can also use a standalone 5V USB power supply when not connected to PC

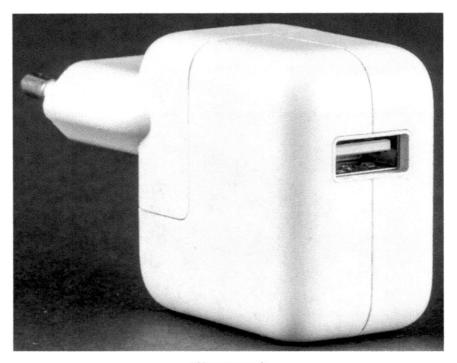

USB power supply

DC power jack

We can also power Arduino board through the DC Power jack.
We can use a 9 to 12V DC, 250mA or more, 2.1mm plug, center-pin positive power adapter. I recommend buying 12V adapter as it will be sufficient for all the power-hungry projects. Following is the image of that:

12V DC power supply

Alternatively, we can use a 9V battery with a DC barrel jack male adapter and battery connector.

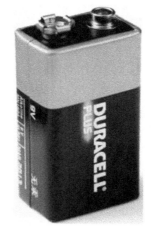

9V battery

Battery connector

DC barrel jack adapter (male)

 You can find all these power supply accessories at any local electronic store or at the online e-stores such as Amazon or eBay.

Arduino IDE installation and setup

Arduino IDE is the open source integrated development environment (IDE) that is used for uploading programs easily to a variety of Arduino boards, clones, and compatibles.

You can visit the Arduino website at https://www.arduino.cc/.

The free software download is located at https://www.arduino.cc/en/Main/Software. Choose the option of Windows Installer. Download the executable installable file. As of writing this book, the filename of the downloaded file is **arduino-1.8.5-windows.exe.** When you are downloading, it might be different as the **Arduino IDE** is under continuous development.

Once download is completed, you can find the file in the Downloads directory of your Web browser. Double-click to execute it. It might ask for the admin credentials. Enter the admin credentials (if needed) and the following window will appear:

Arduino license agreement

Click on I Agree and the Installation Options window will appear:

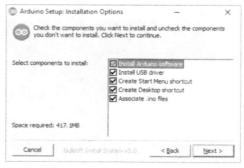

Installation options

Check all the checkboxes and click on Next. Then, choose the directory where you wish the Arduino IDE is to be installed:

Installation options

Click on Install and the installation will commence. The following is the screenshot of Arduino IDE installation in progress:

Installation in progress

When the installation is in progress, you will be prompted as follows:

Prompt for Linino ports device driver installation

Check the checkbox and click on the Install button.

Once the installation finishes, click on Close.

Arduino IDE is now installed on your PC. You can now find the Arduino IDE Icon on desktop. Double-click on the icon and the following splash screen will appear:

Arduino splash screen

Then, after few moments, the splash screen will disappear, and the Arduino IDE will be displayed on the screen as follows:

Arduino splash screen

On the left-hand side, below the menu bar, we find the shortcuts for the most-used menu options:

Shortcut menu

Let's go through the icons, starting from the left-hand side:
• The first option is Verify/Compile.
• The second option is Upload. This uploads the code to the Arduino board connected to a PC.

• The third option creates and opens a new sketch (the Arduino code file) for editing.
• The fourth and fifth options are Open and Save, respectively.
We will use all these options from the next chapter.
Now, click on File from menu and then click on Preferences:

Invoking the preferences

Setting up the preferences

Congrats! We are now ready for getting started with Arduino programming. From the next chapter, we will start with small snippets of the code for Arduino Uno.

Summary

In this chapter, we familiarized ourselves with the Arduino Uno board and the programming environment. We also set up the Arduino IDE for programming the board.

Exercise for this chapter

Visit all the links mentioned in the chapter and become familiar with the Arduino Uno board, microcontroller chip ATmega328P, and Arduino IDE.

Chapter 4

Writing Programs for Arduino

In Chapter 3, Getting Started with Arduino, we got introduced to the Arduino IDE. We learned how to install it on a Microsoft Windows PC. We also configured it according to our own programming needs. From this chapter onward, we will start program- ming with an Arduino board and IDE. The exercises were very light in the earlier chapters. However, from this chapter onward, we will have many, extensive, and practical exercises for all the concepts we will learn throughout the chapter.

For this chapter, the list of hardware components needed is same as in Chapter 3, Getting Started with Arduino:
• A Windows PC with an Internet connection
• An Arduino Uno microcontroller or a compatible clone
• A USB male A to male B cable
• A DC power supply for Arduino
• 9V DC battery, 9V Battery Connector, and 2.1 mm DC barrel jack adapter (male)
• A USB power supply

In Chapter 3, Getting Started with Arduino, we had a very brief introduction to the all the components aforementioned. In this chapter, we will learn how to use them in detail.

Our very first Arduino program

Let's work with our very first Arduino program. Connect the Arduino Uno or compati-ble clone to the PC with the USB cable supplied with it. Refer to the following image:

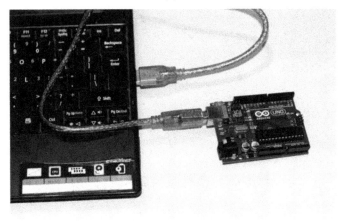

Arduino Uno clone connected to a laptop with USB cable

Once connected and when the PC/laptop is powered on, the power LED on the Arduino Uno board will glow, indicating that the board is in ON state. Now, it is the time to verify whether the Windows OS identifies and recognizes the board. Go to **Control Panel** and then open the **Device Manager** window as follows:

Device Manager screen in Windows Control Panel

Check the Ports (COM and LPT) section in the Device Manager. This way we can know what port the Arduino board is connected to. In my case, it is COM3. It is highlighted in the preceding screenshot. It could be different in your computer.

With all this preparation, we are now ready to start programming for Arduino. Well! Let's first get started with understanding the very structure and style of Arduino programs. An Arduino program is called sketch. In the Arduino community, the terms program, code, and sketch are used interchangeably. A sketch file is saved with **.ino** extension.

With Arduino connected to the PC, open the Arduino IDE by either from the Windows Menu or double-clicking on the Desktop icon. The following window will open:

An Arduino sketch

When we open Arduino IDE, it opens a blank sketch ready to be programmed. Let's try some programming.

Arduino IDE comes with a large number of example sketches. They can be found under the Examples option in the File menu. We will begin programming with very basic sketch. It's similar to Hello World! program in conventional programming. Go to theFile menu. Navigate to **Examples** ->**Basics** ->**Blink.** It will open an example program **Blink.ino** as follows:

```
// the setup function runs once when you press reset or power the
board
void setup() {

// initialize digital pin LED_BUILTIN as an output.
pinMode(LED_BUILTIN, OUTPUT);
}

// the loop function runs over and over again forever
void loop() {

digitalWrite(LED_BUILTIN, HIGH);    // turn the LED on (HIGH is
the voltage level)

delay(1000);                        // wait for a second

digitalWrite(LED_BUILTIN, LOW);     // turn the LED off by making
the voltage LOW
delay(1000);                        // wait for a second
}
```

We know that Pin 13 of Arduino UNO board is connected to a built-in LED. Thepreceding sketch makes that LED blink repeatedly. Let's understand how this sketch works.

The double slash (//) stands for the beginning of the single-line comment. The code enclosed by setup()is executed once. And, the code enclosed by loop() is executed repeatedly once setup() is run.

In setup(), pinMode() is used to set the mode of the pin mentioned. We can configure a pin either as an input or an output. The first argument to this is the number of pins to be configured. On the Uno, Mega, and Zero,it is attached to digital pin 13; on MKR1000, it is attached to digital pin 6. LED_BUILTIN is always set to the correct LED pin independent of which board is used.

In loop(), digitalWrite() writes HIGH (5V or 3.3V, 5V for Arduino Uno) or LOW (0V) on the specified output pin. delay() pauses the program for specified amount of milliseconds.

To summarize the preceding program, in setup(), we are initiating the pin 13 to the OUTPUT mode. In loop(), we are turning the pin 13 LED on and off alternatingly with the delay of a second between each action.

Let's see how to compile and upload this code to the Uno board we have.

Go to the Tools menu and click on the Boards options. Then, select "Arduino/Genuino Uno." Refer to the following screenshot:

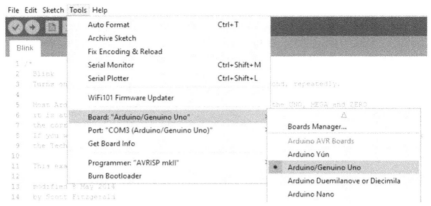

Selecting the correct board for sketch upload

We already know how to verify the COM port Arduino is connected to through the Device Manager in Windows Control Panel. We can verify this from within the Arduino IDE itself. Click on Tools and then onPort: "COM3 (Arduino/ Genuino Uno)." It should show the same port as we saw in the Device Manager.

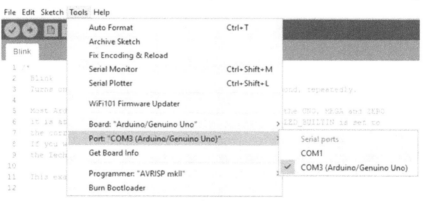

9V battery

Once we select the correct board and verify the port, we can compile the sketch. These two steps are mandatory for the sketch to be uploaded correctly to any board. So, if we are using different boards, we can select the appropriate board from the **Tools** -> **Board menu option**. Additionally, we can click on **Tools** -> **Get Board Info** menu option to see the board information.

The board information

With all the checks done, we can compile the code with the **Sketch** ->**Compile** menu option. Remember that, in Chapter 3, Getting Started with Arduino, we had enabled the verbosity during the compile and upload operations. The bottom part of the IDE is the console output for compile and upload operations. If the compile is successful, then it should show the following message:

Compile success message

Now, we can upload the sketch. Use the **Sketch** ->**Upload** menu option to upload the sketch to the board. The success message is as follows:

Upload success message

Once the sketch is uploaded to the board, the LED connected to pin 13 will start blinking continuously. As we learned earlier, the code in the loop() section runs repeatedly as long as the board is powered.

Alternate ways of powering Arduino

The Arduino board is automatically powered when connected to computer by a USB. There are other ways of powering up the board too. Let's have a look at them too.

USB power

We can power up Arduino through USB power. For that, we either need a USB power bank or a USB power plug. Following is an example of Arduino connected to the USB power plug:

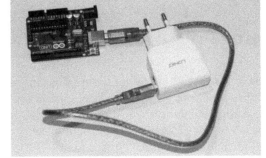

DC power jack

We can either use a DC power supply or a battery to power Arduino through the DC power jack. The following is an image of an Uno board powered through the DC power jack using batteries:

Power pins

We can directly use the 9V battery to power Uno by attaching the + terminal to the VINpin and − terminal to the GND pin. The following schematic represents that:

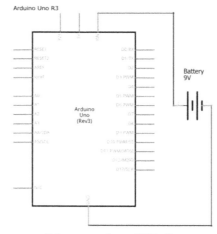

Using power pins and 8V battery

C Programming for Arduino

The Arduino IDE uses a specialized implementation of C language for programming the Arduino boards. It is similar to the regular implementation ofC language. There are added libraries and functionalities for making it work with Arduino boards, derivatives, and compatibles. We will explore many of the libraries and the various added functionalities in the subsequent chapters in the book.

Arduino C data types

As of now, just let's have a look at the various data types available in the C implementation for the Arduino:

Type	Byte length	Range of values
boolean	1	true / false
char	1	−128 to +127
unsigned char	1	0 to 255
byte	1	0 to 255
int	2	−32,768 to 32,767
unsigned int	2	0 to 65,535
word	2	0 to 65,535
long	4	−2,147,483,648 to 2,147,483,647
unsigned long	4	0 to 4,294,967,295
float	4	−3.4028235E+38 to 3.4028235E+38
double	4	−3.4028235E+38 to 3.4028235E+38
string	?	A null terminated reference data type
String	?	An reference data type object
array	?	A sequence of a value type
void	0	A descriptor used with functions when they return nothing

Summary

In this chapter, we familiarized ourselves with the basics of Arduino programming. We will explore more Arduino programming from the next chapter onward by learning how to play with LEDs.

Exercises for this chapter

Following are the exercises for this chapter.
• Power up Arduino by all possible methods mentioned in the chapter.
• Modify the example blink program so that the time for blink is 500 ms.

Chapter 5

LED Programming

Chapter 4, Writing Programs for Arduino, got us started with Arduino programming. We also had a look at the important data types in Arduino C. This chapter will take us a bit further on the journey of Arduino programming. In this chapter, we will get started with the basic knowledge of a few electronic components needed to implement projects in this book. Then, we will proceed toward making simple yet interesting electronic circuits and programming them. We will be learning to make the following circuits:
•An SOS circuit
•Alternate blink circuit
•LED chaser circuits

Let's get introduced to a few new electronic components.

Breadboards

Breadboards or solderless breadboards are the platforms used for the prototyping of electronic circuits. If we have a breadboard and appropriate electronic components, we can make the prototypes of the electronic circuits without for electrical wires, PCBs, and soldering. Breadboards serve as an excellent platform for beginners and veterans alike. Let's have a look at various breadboards and their uses. The following is an image of a breadboard:

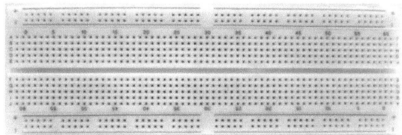
Breadboard

Breadboard socket consists of a block of plastic with many spring clips held under perforations. The clips are known as tie points or contact points. The contact points are used to hold and electrically connect the components. The contact points are arranged in the blocks of strips.
In the preceding image, there are strips marked with + and – signs. They are known as power strips. All the contact points in a row in a block of the terminal strip are electrically connected. Power strips are usually connected to the power sources and provide power to the electrical components mounted on the breadboard.

The other types of blocks are known as the terminal strip blocks. In the preceding image, there are two blocks of terminal strips separated by a groove. The groove acts as a passage for airflow for the integrated circuits (ICs) mounted on the breadboard. Contact points of the terminal strips are used to hold the electrical components and connect them electrically. Unlike the power strips, the contacts points in a column of a terminal strip are electrically connected. In the preceding image, we can see the contact points labeled from A to J row-wise and from 0 to 60 column-wise. The group of contact points A0, B0, C0, D0, and E0 is electrically connected. Thus, the contact points in terminal strip are arranged in groups of five.

The preceding is often called as the full-sized breadboard. There is other variant too. It is called as 400-point breadboard. The following is an image of a 400-point bread-board:

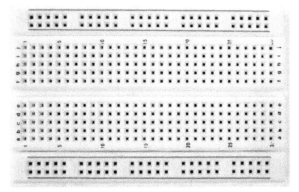

400-point breadboard

Electrically, this is similar to it bigger cousin. The following PCB corresponds to the electrical connections corresponding to a 400-point breadboard:

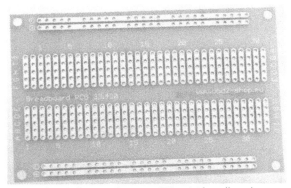

Electrical connections on a 400-point breadboard

The preceding breadboards are frequently used in electronic prototyping. There is a smaller version of breadboard that can be used in small places where space is limited, for example, the circuitry for a wheeled educational robot.The following is an image of this mini breadboard(also known as breadboard without power strips):

Minibreadboard

Also, all the preceding breadboards have a common feature. The have a self-adhesive strip in their rear side so that they can be placed securely when needed. However, once placed, it is difficult to remove the breadboard. So, use this feature wisely.

Jumper wires

We have seen breadboards. We know that the contact points are arranged in the groups, and all contact points within a group are electrically connected. We can connect two contact points that belong to different groups, by a wire. However, connecting them with a wire is a tedious task as we need to find right wire, cut it, and then we need to peel the insulation off from its ends. There is a simple alternative to that. It is known as jumper cables. The following is an image of group of male-to-male jumper cables:

Male-to-male jumper cables

The following image is a female-to-female jumper cable:

Female-to-female jumper cables

The following image is a male-to-female jumper strip. The cables can be separated from the strip and used individually.

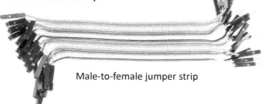

Male-to-female jumper strip

Resistors

Resistors offer resistance to the current. They are often used to limit the amount of current flow or to divide the voltage. In this chapter, we will use the resistor for dividing the voltage. We will use axial-lead resistors that are suitable for use with the breadboards. The following image shows the photograph of a resistor and the electrical symbol for resistor:

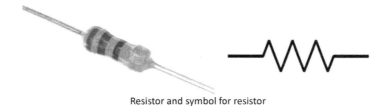

Resistor and symbol for resistor

The resistance of a resistor is color-coded on it. In this chapter, we will use all the 470 ohm resistors.

LED

LED means light-emitting diodes. A diode is an electrical component that allows the current to flow only one way. LEDs glow when current flows through them. The following is image of a bunch of LEDs and the symbol for an LED:

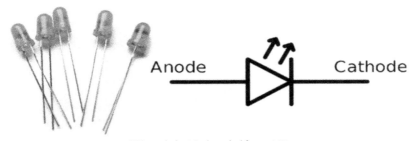

LEDs and electrical symbol for an LED

LEDs can emit light of different colors depending on the material they are made of. The have two leads. The longer lead is known as anode and the smaller lead is known as cathode. The anode is to be connected to the + terminal and the cathode must be connected to the – or ground terminal in a circuit for the current to flow from an LED.

Our very first Arduino circuit

In Chapter 4, Writing Programs for Arduino, we saw an Arduino C program, and if you have whole-heartedly completed the exercise, we can also say that we have made few minor changes to that program. The following is the original program:

```
// the setup function runs once when you press reset or power the
board
void setup() {
// initialize digital pin LED_BUILTIN as an output.
pinMode(LED_BUILTIN, OUTPUT);
}

// the loop function runs over and over again forever
void loop() {
digitalWrite(LED_BUILTIN, HIGH);    // turn the LED on (HIGH is
the voltage level)
delay(1000);                        // wait for a second
digitalWrite(LED_BUILTIN, LOW);     // turn the LED off by making
the voltage LOW
delay(1000);                        // wait for a second
}
```

We know that it is used to continuously blink the built-in LED. We can make an external LED blink using the same program. The following is the close-up photograph of the circuit I made for it:

LED blink circuit

Now, it very difficult to understand how to build the circuit using the photograph. So, we will use circuit diagrams for illustrating the circuits. I use opensource software known as Fritzing to draw the circuit diagram. We will see the breadboard circuit diagram and the schematics of the circuit.The following is the breadboard view of the circuit:

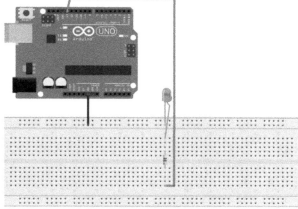

Breadboard view of the circuit

We are connecting the anode of the LED to Pin 13 of the Uno board. We are also connecting the cathode to one of the GND pins of Uno through a 470 ohm resistor. The following is the schematic:

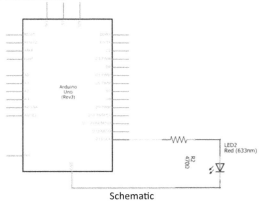

Schematic

When we prepare the circuit and power up the Arduino Uno board, the LED starts blinking.

Morse code SOS

Morse code consists of dots and dashes. It is one of the simplest encoding techniques used for communication. Characters are encoded with dots and dashes. Morse code can be transmitted over many mediums such as audio, electrical pulse, and optical medium. We will use the same LED circuit built for the previous demo for this. We will blink the LED to represent dashes and dots. The blink for long duration means the dash. And, the blink for short duration is a dot. The following is the code for the same:

```
int led = 13;
void setup() // run once, when the sketch starts
{
  pinMode(led, OUTPUT); // sets the digital pin as output
}
void loop()
{
  // Morse for S
  flash(200);
  flash(200);
  flash(200);
  delay(300);

  // Morse for O
  flash(500);
  flash(500);
  flash(500);

  // Morse for S
  flash(200);
  flash(200);
  flash(200);
  delay(1000);
}
void flash(int duration)
{
  digitalWrite(led, HIGH);
  delay(duration);
  digitalWrite(led, LOW);
  delay(duration);
}
```

The Morse code for the character S is three consecutive dots.And, the Morse code for the character O is three consecutive dashes. We have written the code for SOS message. It is an internationally agreed upon signal, which indicates distress. If one is caught in anemergency and potentially life-threatening situation and wants to send a distress signal over a radio, audio, or visual medium, then (s)he can send sequence of three dots followed by three dashes and three dots again.

Let's have a look at the code in detail. We are writing a custom function flash() for creating dashes and dots. It accepts the duration as an argument and keeps the LED connected to pin 13 ON for the duration. The amount of duration the LED is ON determines whether it is a dot or dash. I am using 200 ms for dot and 500 ms for dash. In the loop(), flash() is repeatedly called to create an SOS message. There is a delay of 1 s between two messages. Also, there is a gap of 300 ms between first S and O signal so that the characters can be distinguished easily. When powered up, the LED will flash to send an SOS message visually.

Alternate blink circuit and program

In the previous example, we built the circuit and customized the code. For this example, we will extend the earlier example. Modify the earlier circuit as follows:

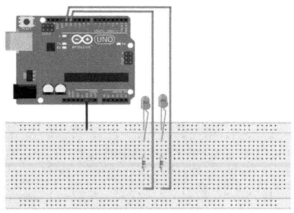

Modified blink circuit

Here, we are connecting an addition LED to Pin 12 of the Uno through a 470 ohm resistor.The following is the schematic of the preceding circuit:

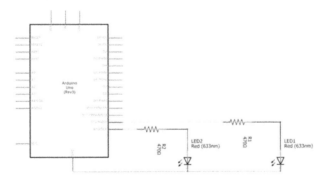

Alternate blinkschematic

Now, we want the LED to blink alternatively. This means that when a LED is ON, then the other should be OFF and vice versa. We need to modify the code for this as follows:

```
int led1 = 13;
int led2 = 12;

void setup()
{
  pinMode(led1, OUTPUT);
```

```
  pinMode(led2, OUTPUT);
}

void loop()
{
  // Turn on the led1, turn off led2
  digitalWrite(led1, HIGH);
  digitalWrite(led2, LOW);
  delay(1000);
  // Turn on the led2, turn off led1
  digitalWrite(led1, LOW);
  digitalWrite(led2, HIGH);
  delay(1000);
}
```

In the preceding code, we are configuring Pins 12 and 13 as output. Then, in loop(), we are alternately turning them ON and OFF. Once we power up the Uno board, then we can see the lights blinking or flashing alternately.

We can also use more sophisticated code to realize the output of the preceding code. Have a look at the program as follows:

```
long counter;
int led1, led2;

void setup()
{
  pinMode(12, OUTPUT);
  pinMode(13, OUTPUT);
  counter = 0;
}

void loop()
{
  if (counter % 2 == 0)
  {
    led1 = 13;
    led2 = 12;
  }
  else
  {
    led1 = 12;
    led2 = 13;
  }

  digitalWrite(led1, HIGH);
  digitalWrite(led2, LOW);
  delay(1000);
  counter = counter + 1;
}
```

In the preceding program, setup() is same as the earlier example. Additionally, we are initializing a count variable counter to 0. In the loop() section, based on the current value of the modulus of counter, we are deciding which LED to turn ON and which one to turn OFF. Finally, we are incrementing the counter. The output is same as the previous example; the LEDs blink alternatively. But, here we demonstrated more complex features of Arduino C programming. We will proceed like this throughout the entire book, that is, adding more and more complexity to the code and circuits on the incremental basis.

LED chaser example

Let's make the earlier example more interesting (and hence more complex)! Add few more LEDs and resistors to the circuit to make it as follows:

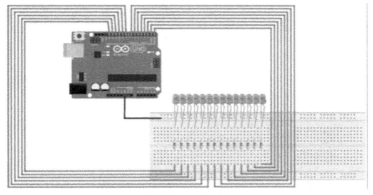

LED chaser circuit

We are using 13 LEDs here. All the digital I/O lines are occupied this way. Let's have some fun with them. Have a look at the following program:

```
int counter;

void setup()
{
  counter = 14;
  for(int i=0; i<counter; i++)
    pinMode(i, OUTPUT);
}

void loop()
{
  for(int i=0; i<counter; i++)
    flash(i, 20);
```

```
}

void flash(int led, int duration)
{
   digitalWrite(led, HIGH);
   delay(duration);
   digitalWrite(led, LOW);
   delay(duration);
}
```

This is our very first example using for loop in Arduino C programming. In setup(), we are configuring all the LEDs as outputs one by one. We have modified the flash() function from the SOS example to accept the LED number as an argument. It still plays the same role of blinking a LED for the given duration. In loop(), we are using for loop to blink each LED once. Thus, at any given instance, only a single LED will blink. All LEDs will blink one after another in the visual series, creating a chaser effect.

Now, the circuit that we built is a multi-purpose circuit, and it can be programmed to create a variety of effects based on the timing when individual LEDs blink. The next few programs will demonstrate this versatility of the circuit we built.

long counter;

```
void setup()
{
   counter = 14;
   for(int i=0; i<counter; i++)
      pinMode(i, OUTPUT);
}

void loop()
{
   for(int i=0; i<counter; i++)
   {
      flash(i, 40);
      if(i<counter)
         flash(i-1,20);
   }
}

void flash(int led, int duration)
{
   digitalWrite(led, HIGH);
   delay(duration);
   digitalWrite(led, LOW);
   delay(duration);
}
```

We just modified the earlier example, and in the each iteration of the for loop, we are flashing two adjacent LEDs one after another.

Let's make it more interesting and flash 3 LEDs consecutively in each iteration. We just need to change the loop() in preceding program as follows:

```
void loop()
{
   for(int i=0; i<counter; i++)
   {
      flash(i, 40);
      if(i<counter)
         flash(i-1,20);
         flash(i-2,10);
   }
}
```

Till now, we experienced only the one-way chaser effect. Now, we will experience the chaser effect in both directions. The following program will have a single chaser visually traverse all the LEDs in both the directions:

```
int counter, led;

void setup()
{
   counter = 14;
   for(int i=0; i<counter; i++)
      pinMode(i, OUTPUT);
}

void loop()
{
   led=0;
   for(int i=0; i<27; i++)
   {
      flash(led, 20);
      if(i<counter-1)
         led++;
      else
         led--;
   }
}

void flash(int led, int duration)
{
   digitalWrite(led, HIGH);
   delay(duration);
   digitalWrite(led, LOW);
   delay(duration);
}
```

Finally, to simulate two chasers always traveling in the opposite direction, write the following code:

```
int counter;
```

```
void setup()
{
  counter = 14;
  for(int i=0; i<counter; i++)
    pinMode(i, OUTPUT);
}

void loop()
{
  for(int i=0; i<counter; i++)
  {
    dualflash(i, 13-i, 20);
  }
}

void dualflash(int led1, int led2, int duration)
{
  digitalWrite(led1, HIGH);
  digitalWrite(led2, HIGH);
  delay(duration);
  digitalWrite(led1, LOW);
  digitalWrite(led2, LOW);
  delay(duration);
}
```

So far, we have implemented five programs for the chaser. I have implemented more ideas for chaser circuits. I am adding them as the part of the exercise section of this book.

Summary

In this chapter, we learned about the basic electronic components such as breadboards, LEDs, and jumpers. We also learned to create few interesting circuits and program them with Arduino C. For more understanding on this chapter, please finish the exercise listed in the next section.

In the next chapter, we will understand how to handle digital and analog inputs. We will also explore a few more functions in the Arduino C library. We will extend the existing projects by introducing inputs to them and explore a few new projects that will use the new concepts.

Exercises for this chapter

The following are the exercises for this chapter. Please complete them to expand your understanding about the concepts learned in this chapter. I have included hints for a few of them.

• Change the duration of the dots and dashes in the SOS program.

• For the chaser circuit, write a program (or rather make a changes in the existing program), which will make all the LEDs blink at the same time. (Hint: Use two separate for loops in the loop() section.)

• Modify the durations of all the chaser code examples to see the effect on the circuit.

• If you have noticed, in the second and the third programs for the chaser circuit, for the first few iterations, we are sending negaative values to the digitalWrite() function in the for loop. Usually, it does not cause any problem. However, in the worst case, it can turn ON a random LED connected to digital I/O pins. We can handle this scenario by adding lines if((i-1)>0) and if((i-2)>0) to the code. Add these conditions to the code to ensure no negative value is passed to the digitalWrite() function.

• Try to arrange the LEDs in the circuit for chaser programs in circular fashion on the breadboard.

• If you are comfortable with printed circuit boards (PCBs), try to create your own PCB for the chaser circuit.

Chapter 6

Programming with Push Buttons

In Chapter 5, LED Programming, we learned how to use LEDs for creating a few inter-esting circuits. We also created and programmed an amazing circuit – the LED chaser circuit.

This short chapter is dedicated to an important electronic component – the push button. In this chapter, we will learn the basics of the push button. Then, we will combine our cumulative learning to create few amazing projects.

Push buttons

Breadboards or solderless breadboards are the platforms used for the prototyping of All of us are familiar with the electric switches. Switches are electrical components (or rather devices) that can turn the supply of electric current ON and OFF to a circuit. It means a switch opens or closes an electric circuit. Push buttons are special type of switches that fall under the category of momentary switches. This means that they close the circuit only when they are pushed.

The following is an image of a few breadboard-friendly push buttons:

Push buttons

As we can see, the preceding push buttons have four legs (or contact points) for the ease of use with the breadboard. You must be wondering why four contact points instead of two like regular switches. The following electric symbol for the breadboard push button speaks for itself and answers the question,

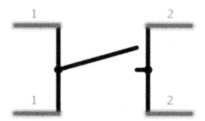

Electrical symbol for the pushbutton

The following image depicts the pushbutton mounted on a breadboard:

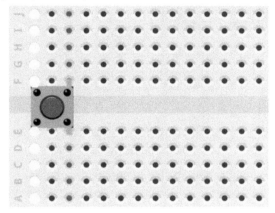

Pushbutton on a breadboard

I have highlighted the electrically connected contact points with same colors. A push button, when not pressed (open state), connects the group of contact points in a row on the both sides of the central groove of the breadboard. In the preceding image, the connected points are marked with the same color. When we press the pushbutton, it connects all the points connected to its legs and closes the circuit.

We can directly connect a push button between an LED and current source. It will be straightforward, yet an interesting exercise. However, it's not the most clever or efficient way to use a push button when we have Arduino. In this chapter, we will focus on programmability of Arduino to use pushbuttons. We will create a couple of simple, yet interesting circuits based on the pushbutton, LEDs, and Arduino. So, let's get started!

Concept of the pull-up resistor

To use the pushbutton as an input device, we need to connect it to one of the programmable pin of the Uno board. However, the there is a problem associated with this. If there is nothing else connected to the pushbutton and the digital I/O pin of Arduino, there is no way to determine whether the signal is HIGH or LOW. This is known as floating and is referred to as the unknown state. There are a couple of techniques to prevent this. We will have a look at one of the most commonly used techniques. It is called as the pull-upresistor.A pull-up resistor is a high-value resistor (I am using 10K for our experiments). Its one end is connected to the 5V supply, and the other end is connected to the push button and to Arduino digital I/O pin. The circuit diagram is as follows:

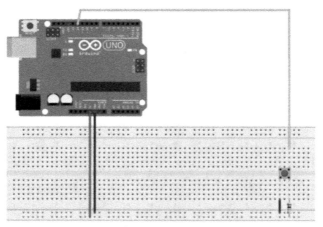

Push button as an input

The following is the circuit schematic for the preceding diagram:

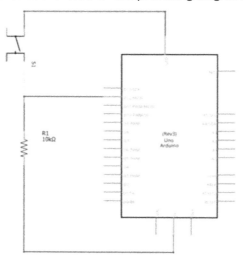

Circuit schematics for the push button as an input

Assemble the preceding circuit. When the push button is in open state (not pressed), the digital pin receives a constant, yet very small amount of current and its state is HIGH. When we push the button, the current takes the path of least resistance and flows to the ground through the GND pin. Thus, the digital pin is LOW. So, this is how we can detect a keypress.

The circuit is the hardware component. We need to program it with the IDE. Let's see a couple of ways we can program it. Consider the following simple program:

```
// Program Constants
const int buttonPin = 12;
const int ledPin =   13;

// Variables
int buttonState = 0;

void setup()
{
   pinMode(ledPin, OUTPUT);
   pinMode(buttonPin, INPUT_PULLUP);
}

void loop()
{
   // Read button state
   buttonState = digitalRead(buttonPin);

   // If button is pressed...
   if (buttonState == LOW)
       digitalWrite(ledPin, HIGH);
   else
       digitalWrite(ledPin, LOW);

   delay(100);

}
```

In the preceding program, we're using the built-in LED connected to digital pin 13 of the Uno board. In the setup() section, we are configuring Pin 12 as INPUT_PULLUP. In the loop() section, digitalRead() is used to detect whether an input pin is HIGH or LOW. As we know, the logic of detecting the keypress is inverted because when the pushbutton is pressed, the pin is LOW. The if statement is used to detect the keypress and to change the state of the LED. The LED glows as long as the button is pressed. Now, we can modify this code such that the LED will persist its state till the next keypress occurs. This means that, if the LED is glowing and you push and release the button, the LED will be OFF. Also, when the LED is OFF and we again push and release the button, the LED will be ON again. We just need to make small changes to the code as follows:

```
// Program Constants
const int buttonPin = 12;
const int ledPin =   13;

// Variables
```

```
int buttonState = 0;
int status = 0;

void setup()
{
  pinMode(ledPin, OUTPUT);
  pinMode(buttonPin, INPUT_PULLUP);
}

void loop()
{
  // Read button state
  buttonState = digitalRead(buttonPin);

  // If button is pressed...
  if (buttonState == LOW)
  {

    // Check if the LED is OFF
    if ( status == 0)
    {
      digitalWrite(ledPin, HIGH);
      status = 1;
    }
    else if ( status == 1)
    {
      digitalWrite(ledPin, LOW);
      status = 0;
    }
  }
  delay(200);

}
```

In the preceding code, we just added a status variable to store the state of the circuit. The status variable is inverted every time we press the pushbutton, and based on the status variable, we change the LED's state.

These were the simplest use cases of the push button. Let's have a look at a couple of more complex examples of the use cases of the push button.

Traffic light

Let's create a simple traffic light system with the pushbutton, LEDs, and resistors. The following is the circuit:

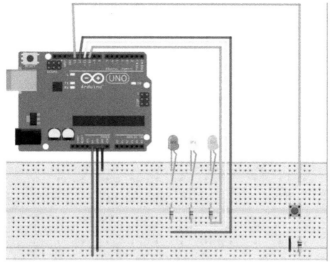
A traffic light system

In the preceding circuit, the resistor used with the button is a 10K resistor. The resistors used with traffic lights LEDs are 470 ohm resistors. We are connecting the pushbutton to digital pin 13. I am connecting red, yellow (an orange/amber color would also do), and green LEDs with the pins 12, 11, and 10 respectively. This completes the circuit.

Let's have a look at the working of the traffic light in real life. The following is the convention used in UK and most of the former UK colonies:

• Red: Stop immediately
• Red and yellow: Stop, soon it will turn green
• Green: Go
• Yellow: Stop unless it is not safe to do so

Let's write the code for the same:

```
int red = 12;
int yellow = 11;
int green = 10;

int button = 13;

int buttonState = 0;
int state = 0;

void setup()
{
  pinMode(red, OUTPUT);
  pinMode(yellow, OUTPUT);
  pinMode(green, OUTPUT);

  pinMode(button, INPUT_PULLUP);
```

```
}

void loop()
{
  buttonState = digitalRead(button);

  if (buttonState==LOW)
  {
    if (state == 0)
    {
      LightsOn(HIGH, LOW, LOW);
      state = 1;
    }
    else if (state == 1)
    {
      LightsOn(HIGH, HIGH, LOW);
      state = 2;
    }
    else if (state == 2)
    {
      LightsOn(LOW, LOW, HIGH);
      state = 3;
    }
    else if (state == 3)
    {
      LightsOn(LOW, HIGH, LOW);
      state = 0;
    }
    delay(1000);
  }
}
void LightsOn(int redStatus, int yellowStatus, int greenSta-
tus)
{
  digitalWrite(red, redStatus);
  digitalWrite(yellow, yellowStatus);
  digitalWrite(green, greenStatus);
}
```

In the preceding code, we are cycling through the states of the traffic signal discussed in the preceding bullet points. We are changing the state on the keypress, even of the pushbutton. We are modularizing the operation to turn ON and OFF the entire set of LEDs using the custom-defined function LightsOn().

Visualizing random numbers generation

Let's use LEDs and the pushbutton for visualizing the random number generation.

Have a look at the following circuit:

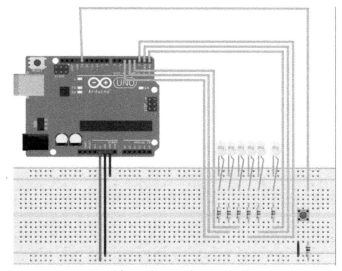

Circuit for random number visualization

We're connecting the digital pin 12 to the push button and pins 0 through 5 to LEDs. The following is the code for the random numbers:

```
int button = 13;
int buttonState = 0;
long randomNumber;

void setup()
{
  for ( int i = 0; i < 6; i++ )
    pinMode(i, OUTPUT);

  pinMode(button, INPUT_PULLUP);
  randomSeed(42);
}

void loop()
{
  buttonState = digitalRead(button);

  if (buttonState==LOW)
  {
    randomNumber = random(0, 6);

    for ( int i = 0; i < 6; i++ )
```

```
    {
      if( i <= randomNumber )
        digitalWrite(i, HIGH);
      else
        digitalWrite(i, LOW);
    }

  }
  delay(200);
}
```

In the preceding code, the function call randomSeed() in setup() initializes the random number generator. In the loop() section, the built-in function random() generates a random number within the given range. We are turning ON the number of LEDs equal to generated random number on a keypress.

Summary

In this short chapter, we learned in detail how to use and program a pushbutton with the Arduino Uno board. We also created three circuits and wrote four programs for those in detail. Push buttons are very important because many industrial applications use them as a preferred method of input. One of the most used day-to-day examples of usage of pushbuttons is the calculator keypad,

A calculator keypad

Also, other examples of pushbuttons include the keypads of remote controllers of TVs and video games, and the keyboards of computers and electronic musical instruments. In the later part of this book, we will work with the remote controls, keypads, and music along with Arduino.

Exercises for this chapter

I hope you have enjoyed creating the chaser circuit from Chapter 5, LED Programming. It will be an interesting exercise to add a level of interactivity to the chaser circuit using the pushbutton. Let me explain how to accomplish that. We know that there is a duration component involved in designing the chaser effect. We can add a pushbutton and program it such that, on keypress, it cycles through various amounts of durations for the chasers. And, after reaching the highest delay, it should resume from the beginning.

Chapter 7

Analog Inputs and Various Buses

We learned to work with digital inputs and analog switches in Chapter 6, Programming with Push Buttons. We also created few real-life and a bit more complex examples. In this chapter, we will learn how to handle analog inputs. We will also learn various communication mechanisms and buses Arduino has for data exchange between with other devices. First, we will get started with serial data transfer. Then, we will learn how we can use it for debugging the Arduino programs. We will then move on to handling analog inputs. Finally, we will have an overview of SPI and I2C buses in Arduino.

Serial data transfer

There are various ways we can transfer data between electronic devices or components within an electronic system. The most common ways are parallel data transfer and serial data transfer. The following is a diagram of a parallel data transfer arrangement:

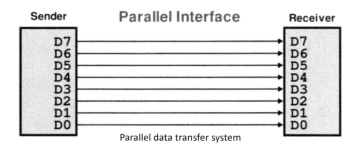

Parallel data transfer system

As we can see in the preceding diagram, for every bit in an 8-byte word of data, there is a dedicated bus line. In the preceding diagram, the bus line isunidirectional. This means that the bus carries the data only in one direction. Often, the bus lines are bidirectional and are capable of carrying the data in both directions.

An advantage of parallel bus is that we can transmit multiple bits simultaneously. The drawback is that we need to have extra bus lines, which might take up a lot of space and hardware.

The other more frequently used arrangement is serial data transfer, also known as serial communication or serial bus. The following diagram depicts a unidirectional serial communication system where the most significant bit is transmitted and received first:

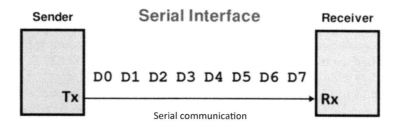

Serial communication

The sender-side end is known as Tx (transmission) and the receiver side end is known as Rx (receiver/reception). For the preceding system to be bidirectional, both the devices have Tx and Rx pins. Tx of a device is always connected to Rx of the other device and viceversa, to facilitate communication. We can use serial bus in synchronous and asynchronous modes. For synchronous transmission, there could be additional pins for synchronization control and timing signals. There are many implementations of synchronous serial communication. Prominent examples include RS232, SPI, and I2C.The following is the pin diagram of a RS232-style connector:

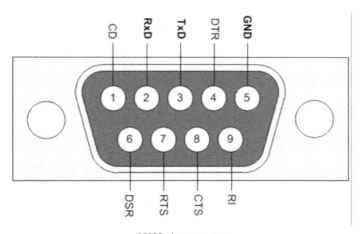

RS232 pin connector

In earlier days of computing, RS232 ports were ubiquitous. Almost every IBM PC and clones had them. The standard I/O services, such as keyboard, mouse, and printers could be connected to a PC. Many modems were also RS232-compatible. Though RS232 is still popular, no modern motherboards have an RS232 port due to their declining use in PCs. However, they remain a popular choice for other industry segments such as embedded systems.

Arduino Serial

Arduino boards have Arduino Serial for communication between them and other devices such as a desktop computer. Arduino Serial is an asynchronous bus that uses only Tx and Rx pins for communication. The Arduino Uno board uses Pin 0 as Rx and Pin 1 as Tx for serial communication. It can also use the USB port for serial communication with a computer as the pins are connected to the board's built-in USB-to-serial adapter. When we use serial communication via Pins 0 and 1 or USB, we cannot use Pins 0 and 1 in the digital I/O mode.

The serial pins use TTL (transistor-transistor-logic) level of 5V for Arduino Uno. It is really not a good idea to connect them with RS232, as RS232 uses ±12V logic levels. It will fry the board damaging it beyond repair, thus rendering it useless.

Getting started with Arduino Serial

Let's get started with Arduino Serial. We will see a simple program that is used for blinking an LED and also printing the status of the LED on the screen.The Arduino IDE has tools to visualize the communication with the serial port and pins. The most used is the Serial Monitor. It can be used when an Arduino board is connected to the computer through a USB. It can be found under the Tools menu option in the menubar. Let's see how we can use the Serial Monitor to debug a program. Let's get started with the simplest example. I hope you remember our very first Arduino program for LED blink. Let's modify it to print the status of the LED on the Serial Monitor:

```
void setup() {
  // initialize digital pin LED_BUILTIN as an output.
  pinMode(LED_BUILTIN, OUTPUT);
  Serial.begin(9600);
}

// the loop function runs over and over again forever
void loop() {
  digitalWrite(LED_BUILTIN, HIGH);   // turn the LED on (HIGH
is the voltage level)
  Serial.println("LED ON");
  delay(1000);                       // wait for a second
  digitalWrite(LED_BUILTIN, LOW);    // turn the LED off by
making the voltage LOW
  delay(1000);                       // wait for a second
  Serial.println("LED OFF");
}
```

In the preceding program, in the **setup()** section, with **Serial.begin(9600)**, we are initializing serial communication at the baud rate of 9,600. In the **loop()** section, we are using **Serial.println()** to print data in human-readable ASCII format. Upload the sketch to an Arduino Uno board and keep the board connected to the computer. Open the Serial Monitor. It will show the output as follows:

Serial Monitor

You will also notice that one of the two LEDs besides Pin 13 LED is labeled as Tx, and it also blinks everytime something is printed on the Serial Monitor. The following is the a close-up photo:

Tx and Rx LEDs

For the preceding coding example, only Tx LED will blink.

Let's use serial communication for input. Consider the following code:

```
void setup()
{
    // initialize digital pin LED_BUILTIN as an output.
    pinMode(LED_BUILTIN, OUTPUT);
```

```
        Serial.begin(9600);
}

// the loop function runs over and over again forever
void loop()
{
  if(Serial.available() > 0)
  {
    char letter = Serial.read();
    if(letter == '1')
    {
digitalWrite(LED_BUILTIN, HIGH);    // turn the LED on (HIGH
is the voltage level)
      Serial.println("LED ON");
      delay(1000);
    }
    else if(letter == '0')
    {
      digitalWrite(LED_BUILTIN, LOW);    // turn the LED off
by making the voltage LOW
      delay(1000);                       // wait for a
      second
      Serial.println("LED OFF");
    }
  }
}
```

Serial.available() checks the number of bytes available for reading from the serial port. Serial.read() reads the data over the serial stream. Run the preceding code and open the Serial Monitor. In the textbox located at top of the Serial Monitor window, type 1 and then click on the Send button. The built-in LED for pin 13 will be ON. In the same way, you can turn it off by sending it to0. This is how we can use serial communication via built-in USB-to-serial of Arduino Uno. In the later part of this book, we will learn how to use Pins 0 and 1 (Rx and Tx) for the serial communication.

Analog input

In Chapter 6, Programming with Push Buttons, we learned how to work with the digital input component (push button) that can be connected to one of the digital I/O pins of Arduino. Digital inputs are pretty much simple as they just have two states, 0 or 1. Analog inputs are a bit more complex, as they offer a variety of values as input. The most common and simplest of analog input components is a potentiometer. It is a resistor with three pins. The middle pin is used as an input to the analog pin of Arduino. Other two pins are used to connect it to the reference voltage and GND pin. The following is an image of a potentiometer:

Potentiometer

There is breadboard-friendly version of potentiometer as follows:

A 10K breadboard potentiometer

Potentiometers are essentially voltage dividers. They divide the reference voltage using built-in variable resistors.
Consider the following circuit diagram:

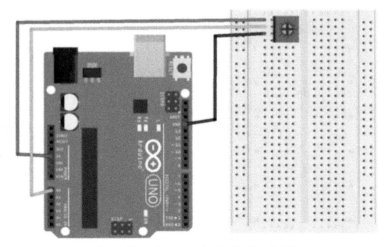

A potentiometer connected to the Uno Pin A0

Connect the middle pin of the potentiometer to Pin A0. Connect one pin to 5V and the remaining to GND. We will use the same circuit for the next couple of coding examples.

We have created the circuit for the analog input. Let's write the code for it:

```
void setup() {
  // initialize serial communication at 9600 bits per second:
  Serial.begin(9600);
}
// the loop routine runs over and over again forever:
void loop() {
  // read the input on analog pin 0:
  int sensorValue = analogRead(A0);
  // print out the value you read:
  Serial.println(sensorValue);
  delay(1);          // delay in between reads for stability
}
```

The code is very easy to understand. There is only one new function analogRead() that we don't know yet. It accepts the analog pin name (A0 to A5 for Uno) or number (0 to 5 for Uno) as an argument. It reads the analog value from the connected device. Arduino's analog pins are connected to a 10-bit analog to digital converter. Resolution of 10 bits means we can have 1,024 distinct values.

Once we upload the sketch to the Uno, we can see it in action. Keep Arduino connected to the computer and open the Serial Monitor. You will be able to see the current reading from the potentiometer. Rotate the knob and you can see the value changing. The following is the Serial Monitor:

Arduino serial output

We can also make it a bit more interesting. From Tools in the menubar, open the Serial Plotter and observe the graph of the analog input:

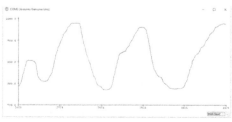

Arduino Serial Monitor

You might have noticed by this time that the value of the input varies from 0 to 1023. We know the reference voltage to the potentiometer. It is +5V. We can determine the voltage level of the analog input by mapping the numbers in the range 0 to 1,023 to the range 0 to +5 as follows:

```
void setup() {
  // initialize serial communication at 9600 bits per second:
  Serial.begin(9600);
}


// the loop routine runs over and over again forever:
void loop() {
  // read the input on analog pin 0:
  int sensorValue = analogRead(A0);
  // Convert the analog reading (which goes from 0 - 1023) to
a voltage (0 - 5V):
  float voltage = sensorValue * (5.0 / 1023.0);
  // print out the value you read:
  Serial.println(voltage);
}
```

Compile and upload the preceding sketch and observe the value of voltage change on Serial Monitor and Plotter.

Also, Arduino IDE has a in-built map() function to map the input range to a custom range. For that, we need to know the range of input values for the Analog pin. We already know that the input range is 0 to 1,023. Let's write a small program to map it from 0 to 255:

```
void setup() {
  // initialize serial communication at 9600 bits per second:
  Serial.begin(9600);
}
// the loop routine runs over and over again forever:
void loop() {
  // read the input on analog pin 0:
  int sensorValue = analogRead(0);
  // Convert the analog reading (which goes from 0 - 1023) to
a voltage (0 - 5V):
  int val = map(sensorValue, 0, 1023, 0, 255);
  // print out the value you read:
  Serial.println(val);
}
```

The map() function accepts five arguments. The first one is the variable to be mapped, the second the third are the input range, and the fourth and fifth are the target range.

In the subsequent chapters, we will be extensively using the analog input to control few parameters in our circuit.

Arduino SPI

SPI stands for **Serial Peripheral Interface (SPI)** bus. It is a type of serial and synchronous bus. It was developed by Motorola in the 1980s. It uses full duplex mode, that is, bidirectional data flow at the same time for data communication. It also uses the master–slave arrangement for control. The SPI bus has the following signals:

• **SCLK or SCK:** Serial Clock (clock output signal from master)
• **MOSI:** Master Output Slave Input (data output signal from master to slave)
• **MISO:** Master Input Slave Output (data output signal from slave to master)
• **SS:** Slave Select (Signal used to select the slave chip/device)

The following is the block diagram of a single master–slave arrangement:

SPI master-slave arrangement

In the preceding diagram, the SPI master is usually the Arduino Uno. The digital Pin 13 of Uno is used for SCK/SCLK, digital Pin 12 is used for MISO, and digital Pin 11 is used for MOSI. We can use any of the remaining digital pins for SS. Usually, by convention, digital Pin 10 is used for SS in single master–slave configuration as it is adjacent to the other SPI pins. However, we can use any digital I/O pin for this function.

The following is an example of multiple independent slaves connected to a master:

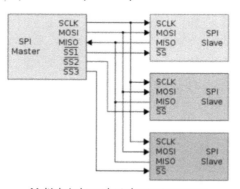

Multiple independent slave arrangement

Also, it is possible to have a single SS signal for multiple slaves. For that, we need to arrange the circuit in daisy chain mode as follows:

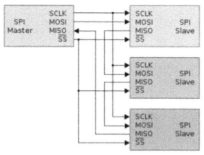

Daisy chain arrangement for many slaves

Many hardware components use SPI as the primary means of communication with Arduino. In the subsequent chapters, we will study those components and their interfacing with Arduino.

Arduino I2C

I2C means inter-integrated circuit. It was invented by Philips semiconductor.It is a type of serial and synchronous bus. We know that asynchronous serial requires only two lines, but we need to agree on data rate (baud rate) for the data exchange. The synchronous serial buses such as SPI are bidirectional and require four lines. However, the major drawback of the SPI is that it can only have a single master device.

I2C eliminates all the drawbacks of the asynchronous serial and SPI and combines their benefits. It requires only two lines, SDA (data line) and SCL (clock line). It can have multiple master nodes, and it is synchronous. It supports very high rate of data transfer. There are many implementations on I2C. Usually, the speeds of generic I2C implementations vary between 100 kHz to 400 kHz. Few specialized implementations support up to 5 MHz rate of data transfer. I2C can support up to 1008 devices connected in the I2C bus.

The details of I2C as a bus and its implementation are not needed much to see I2C in action. We will see that in the subsequent chapters of the book.

In Arduino Uno, SDA and SCL lines are close to the AREF pin. The following image shows the locations of these pins:

Location of Arduino I2C pins

Summary

In this chapter, we learned the basics of serial bus in detail. We learned about its different flavors and learned to work with Arduino serial. We also saw how to use analog pins for the input. We saw the basics of synchronous flavors of serial, I2C and SPI. In the subsequent chapters, we will use these buses to connect a lot of devices to Arduino.

Exercises for this chapter

Complete the following exercise to broaden the understanding of the topics we learned in this book:

In Chapter 6, Programming with Push Buttons, we added a pushbutton to the chaser circuit to control the duration of the LED blink. Modify the original chaser circuit and control the duration of the LED blink, and hence the speed of the chaser using a potentiometer.

Chapter 8

Arduino Ethernet Shield

Till now, we have learned how to interface Arduino with basics electronic components such aspush buttons, LEDs, and potentiometers. We also learned the concept of analog and digital inputs. We know the basics of various buses such asSPI and I2C. We learned in Chapter 1, Basics of Internet of Things,that an IoT-based product or service has a networked microprocessor/microcontroller to collect the data and user inputs with the help of various sensors and I/O devices. As aforementioned, we have familiarized ourselves with Arduino and basics of I/O interfacing to Arduino. We need to focus on the networking part now. So, in this chapter, we will understand and demonstrate how to connect an Arduino to a network and Internet. For that, we will first know what Arduino Ethernet Shield is and how to use itto connect Arduino to Internet.

Arduino shields

Arduino shields are readymade printed circuit boards (PCBs) thatcanbe plugged into Arduino boards to extend the board's functionality. On the official Arduino Products page (https://www.arduino.cc/en/Main/Products), we can find the shields marked in yellow color. The following is the screenshot:

Shields highlighted in yellow color on the Arduino Products page

Remember, these are the only official shields. And, as we know that, the Arduino follows philosophy of opensource hardware, there are many clones of these shields available in the market. You can design even your own shield with the custom functionality.

Arduino Ethernet Shields

Arduino Ethernet Shields, as the name suggests, are used to connect the Arduino to the Ethernet network thatuses the RJ45 connector. There are two versions of the official Arduino shields, **V1R3 (Version 1 Revision 3)** and V2. Ethernet Shield V1R3 is retired and has ceased to be produced. However, many third-party manufacturers still make its clones. Ethernet Shield V2 is the latest one, and as of writing of this book, is in production.

The following is a top-down photograph of the Ethernet Shield V1R3:

Arduino Ethernet Shield V1R3

The following is a top-down photograph of the Ethernet Shield V2:

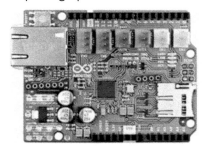
Arduino Ethernet Shield V2

Let's have a look at the specifications of the boards. Bothboards operate on 5V, which is provided by the Arduino board. They connect to the Arduino board via a Serial Peripheral Interface(SPI) (we learned this in the Chapter 7, Analog Inputs and Various Buses) and provide the connection speed of 10/100 Mbps with Ethernet. If the Ethernet network to which the board is connected to is connected to the Internet, then the Arduino can connect to the Internet. Both boards also have a microSD card reader, which we will explore in the subsequent chapters for our IoT experiments.

The essential difference between both boards is that the V1R3 uses the Ethernet controller W5100, which has internal buffer of 16K, and the shield V2 uses W5500,

which has internal buffer of 32K. The shield V2 also has the following Tinkernut socket connectors:
- 2 TinkerKit connectors for two analog inputs (colored in white), connected to A2 and A3.
- 2 TinkerKit connectors for two analog outputs (colored in orange in the middle), connected to PWM outputs on pins D5 and D6.
- 2 TinkerKit connectors for the TWI interface (colored in green with 4 pins), one for input and the other one for output.

Connecting the Arduino Ethernet Shields to Arduino boards

The following is the bottom-up photograph of an Ethernet Shield:

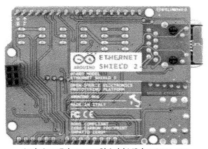

Arduino Ethernet Shield V2 bottom-up

As we can see in the preceding photograph, the shield has male headers and female for connection to the Arduino board. Plug it on the top of theArduino board. Connect the Ethernet RJ-45 cable and also connect the Arduino board to a computer. Refer to the following image:

Arduino Ethernet Shield connected to a Uno board

Once the setup is done, we can move to coding. For using Ethernet Shields,we have to use Arduino Ethernet library and SPI library. The following program demonstrates how an Arduino with Ethernet Shield acquiresan IP address statically:

```
#include <SPI.h>
#include <Ethernet.h>
//#include<Ethernet2.h>
```

```
//Enable the above library if you are using a W5500 based
shield
byte mac[] = {  0xDE, 0xAD, 0xBE, 0xEF, 0xFE, 0xED };
IPAddress ip(192, 168, 2, 170);
void setup() {
  Serial.begin(9600);

  // disable SD card if one in the slot

  pinMode(4,OUTPUT);
  digitalWrite(4,HIGH);
  Serial.println("Starting W5100");

//Serial.println("Starting W5500");
//Enable the above line if you are using a W5500 based shield
  Ethernet.begin(mac,ip);

  Serial.println(Ethernet.localIP());
}
void loop()
{
}
```

Let's understand the preceding program line by line. First, we import the SPI library. Then, if we are using an Ethernet Shield with W5100, we have to use Ethernet.h; if we are using an Ethernet Shield with W5500, we need to use the Ethernet2.h library (I have included it in the code comments). After including the needed libraries, we are allocatting the medium access control (MAC) address and an IP address to the device. If you are using one of the most recently manufactured shields, then the MAC address will be mentioned on a sticker on the shield or the packaging box or the manual. If the MAC address is not provided, we can use any valid random MAC address for our task. Just make sure that if you are using multiple devices, the MAC address should not be repeated. And, the IP address depends on your router settings. Also, you need to make sure that there is no conflict of IP addresses.

 You can use the **nmap** tool to check the allocated IP address to avoid any conflict.

Once done with MAC and IP addresses, we are disabling the SD card module on the shield (we will work with that in the subsequent chapters). Then, we are using the Ethernet.begin() function call to connect the shield to the Ethernet. Finally, the Ethernet.localIP() function call returns the IP address allocated to Arduino.

This is a simplest program to connect to an Ethernet network and to print the IP address. The following is an instance under execution:

```
1  #include <SPI.h>
2  #include <Ethernet.h>
3  //#include<Ethernet2.h>
4  //Enable the above library if you are useing a W5500 based shield
5
6  byte mac[] = {  0xDE, 0xAD, 0xBE, 0xEF, 0xFE, 0xED };
7  IPAddress ip(192, 168, 2, 170);
8  EthernetClient client;
9
10 void setup() {
11   Serial.begin(9600);
12
13   // disable SD card if one in the slot
14   pinMode(4, OUTPUT);
15   digitalWrite(4, HIGH);
16
17   Serial.println("Starting W5100");
18 //Serial.println("Starting W5500");
19 //Enable the above line if you are useing
20   Ethernet.begin(mac, ip);
21
22   Serial.println(Ethernet.localIP());
23 }
24
25 void loop()
26 {
27 }
```

COM3 (Arduino/Genuino Uno)

Starting W5100
192.168.2.170

Done uploading
avrdude done.   Thank you.

First network program with Arduino

The example we just followed is the simplest case of Arduino Ethernet Shield. We will have a look at more complex examples using Arduino Ethernet Shields from the next chapter.

Working with Arduino Ethernet

Every time we want to work with the Ethernet Shield, we need to mount it on the Arduino board. There is an alternative to this. An Arduino board Arduino Ethernet without POE combines the functionality of the Uno board and Ethernet Shield with the W5100 controller in a single package. The link to the Products page on Arduino website is https://store.arduino.cc/usa/arduino-ethernet-rev3-without-poe. The following is a top-down photograph of an Arduino Ethernet without POE:

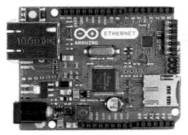

Arduino Ethernet without POE

As we can see, there is no USB port for direct connection to a PC. However, on the top-right side, we can see six serial pins thatcan be connected to a converter thatcan convert serial signals to USB and vice versa. We can use Arduino's USB 2 Serial Converter. You can find it on the Arduino's Products page at https://store.ardui-no.cc/usa/arduino-usb-2-serial-micro. Following is the top-down view of the converter board:

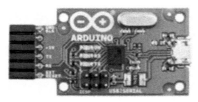

Arduino USB 2 Serial Converter

The following is an image of Arduino Ethernet without POE connected to an Ethernet network and to a computer through the USB 2 Serial Converter:

Arduino Ethernet connected to a PC

In the Arduino IDE, you have to choose the appropriate board from the Tools menu:

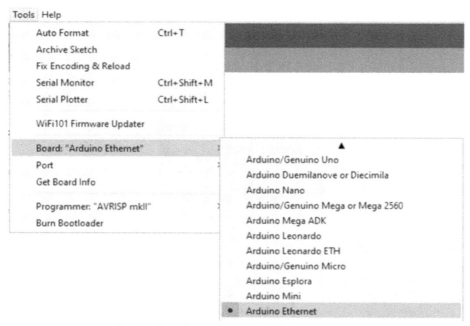

Choosing the Arduino Ethernet board from the Tools menu

Summary

In this chapter, we learned the basics of Ethernet Shields and how to use them to connect to the Arduino boards to the Internet. The chapter is short and crisp to gradually ramp the readers up to IoT. From the next chapter, we will see more complex examples and exercises with Arduino Ethernet Shields.

References

- https://learn.sparkfun.com/tutorials/arduino-shields
- https://www.arduino.cc/en/Main/Products

Exercises for this chapter

Complete the following exercise to broaden the understanding of the topics we learned in this book:
- Visit all the links mentoned in the references. It will give you a good idea about various official and third-party shields.

Chapter 9

Arduino IoT Projects

In Chapter 8, Arduino Ethernet Shield, we learned a few things about Arduino Shields. We learned how we can connect an Arduino Ethernet Shield (based on W5100 or W5500) to connect Arduino to the Internet. We also learned the basics of another Arduino board, Arduino Ethernet without POE. In this chapter, we will see a few more projects based on Internet connectivity with Arduino. We can either use a Uno board with the Ethernet Shield or Arduino Ethernet without POE for the projects in this book.

DHCP demoprogram

In Chapter 8, Arduino Ethernet Shield, we saw how to assign an IP address to an Arduino manually. Now, we will see how to assign an IP address to an Arduino board dynamically. The network management protocol used for assigning an IP address dynamically to any board is Dynamic Host Configuration Protocol (DHCP). When DHCP is to be used, there is always a DHCP server that assumes the task for assigning the IP addresses dynamically to the hosts within the network. In most of the cases, networking devices such as managed switches or routers assume the job of DHCP servers. If you are using corporate or educational networks, then these networks usually have DHCP servers or DHCP-enabled network devices for dynamic allocation of IP addresses.

In this chapter, the very first program we will implement and study is the demo of DHCP. If you remember, in Chapter 8, Arduino Ethernet Shield,I mentioned that we need to provide the MAC address for our Ethernet controller and many shields or Arduino Ethernet boards will have the address printed on a sticker on their back. The following is a photograph of the sticker with printed MAC address on the back of Arduino Ethernet without POE I am using for all of our demos:

Arduino Ethernet board MAC address sticker

To get started, mount the Ethernet Shield to the Arduino Uno board or use the Arduino Ethernet board with USB to Serial converter. Connect the board to a computer and
Ethernet network.

The following is the program for DHCP demo:

```
#include <SPI.h>
#include <Ethernet.h>
byte mac[] = {
    0x90, 0xA2, 0xDA, 0x10, 0x81, 0x42
};
void setup()
{

  Serial.begin(9600);


  if (Ethernet.begin(mac) == 0) {
        Serial.println("Failed  to  configure  Ethernet  using
DHCP");
      for (;;)
         ;
  }

  printIPAddress();
}

void loop()
{
}

void printIPAddress()
{
  Serial.print("My IP address: ");
  for (byte thisByte = 0; thisByte < 4; thisByte++) {
    // print the value of each byte of the IP address:
    Serial.print(Ethernet.localIP()[thisByte], DEC);
    Serial.print(".");
  }

  Serial.println();
}
```

The preceding program is not much different from the IP address printer program
we saw in Chapter 8, Arduino Ethernet Shield. Here, we are passing the MAC
address to Ethernet.begin(), whereas we passed an additional argument of
manual IP address to it in Chapter 8, Arduino Ethernet Shield. The
printIPAddress() function prints the IP address in the decimal format. The
following is the output:

DHCP IP address

Additionally, you can check the active client list from your router's homepage. Even a better way is to use the nmap command. The command one needs to use is **nmap −sn 192.168.2.*** and it will show a list of active clients connected to the network 192.168.2.*. Please check your router's manual to know your subnet address. The following is the output of the command for my network:

NMAP command output

As we can see, in the preceding output, 192.168.2.1 is the IP address of the router I am using. Actually, conventionally, x.y.z.1 is always the IP address of router or managed switch. Also, we can verify Arduino's IP address and also see that it is paired with its MAC address in the program.

To use NMAP, you have to install it. In Linux, just use the package management tool to install it. Then you can run the command in the Terminal. In Windows, you can install the Zenmap GUI and run the command. The preceding screenshot is of the Zenmap GUI running on Windows. For more information, please check https://nmap.org/zenmap/ and https://nmap.org.

Arduino Webclient

We all use web browsers such as Firefox and Chrome. Web browsers are the Web clients that initiate a request to a website, retrieve the requested data, and display it in formatted HTML format. In this section, we will program a simple and Arduino-based Web client that retrieves data from a server and then displays it in the plaintext format.The following is the program:

```
#include <SPI.h>
#include <Ethernet.h>

byte mac[] = { 0x90, 0xA2, 0xDA, 0x10, 0x81, 0x42 };
char server[] = "www.google.com";

IPAddress ip(192, 168, 2, 3);
EthernetClient client;

void setup()
{

  Serial.begin(9600);

  if (Ethernet.begin(mac) == 0)
  {
       Serial.println("Failed  to  configure  Ethernet  using
DHCP");
    Serial.println("Assigning IP address manually");
    Ethernet.begin(mac, ip);
  }

  delay(1000);
  Serial.println("connecting...");

  if (client.connect(server, 80))
  {
    Serial.println("connected");
    client.println("GET /search?q=AshwinPajankar HTTP/1.1");
    client.println("Host: www.google.com");
    client.println("Connection: close");
    client.println();
  }
  else
  {
    Serial.println("connection failed");
  }
}

void loop()
{
  if (client.available())
  {
```

```
    char c = client.read();
    Serial.print(c);
  }

  if (!client.connected())
  {
    Serial.println();
    Serial.println("disconnecting.");
    client.stop();

    while (true);
  }
}
```

The preceding program, in most parts, is similar to the earlier programs. Before setup(), we are declaring an EthernetClient variable. In setup(), first we try to obtain an IP address with DHCP, and if it fails, we assign it manually. Then, we are connecting to theGoogle server on port 80 using client.connect(). client.println() is used to send an HTTP request to the connected server. In the preceding example, we are sending the GET request to the Google server for search of string of my name. In the loop() section, we are reading the response from the server and printing it line by line. Run the preceding example and observe the output.

Arduino telnet chat server

Let's create a simple application of Arduino-based chat server.The following is the code for this:

```
#include <SPI.h>
#include <Ethernet.h>

byte mac[] = { 0x90, 0xA2, 0xDA, 0x10, 0x81, 0x42 };

IPAddress ip(192, 168, 2, 3);
EthernetServer server(23);
boolean alreadyConnected = false;
EthernetClient client;

void setup()
{
  Serial.begin(9600);
  if (Ethernet.begin(mac) == 0)
  {
       Serial.println("Failed to configure Ethernet using
DHCP");
    Serial.println("Assigning IP address manually");
    Ethernet.begin(mac, ip);
  }
```

```
  delay(1000);
  server.begin();
  Serial.print("Chat server address: ");
  Serial.println(Ethernet.localIP());
}

void loop()
{
  client = server.available();
  if (client)
  {
    if (!alreadyConnected)
    {
      client.flush();
      Serial.println("We have a new client");
      client.print("You are connected to ");
      client.println(Ethernet.localIP());
      alreadyConnected = true;
    }
    if (client.available())
    {
      char thisChar = client.read();
      Serial.write(thisChar);
    }
  }
}
```

In the preceding code, we are creating a server at port 23, which is the default port for telnet application/utility. In the setup() section, server.begin() initiates the server. In the loop() section, we are checking whether a client is connected and printing its IP address. And, once the client connects and is available, we are printing the text entered from the client's terminal over the network.

To see the preceding program in the action, upload the code to Arduino and from another computer connect to the Arduino using telnet utility in Windows. Once the other computer is connected to the Arduino, we can check the IP address of connected computer in Arduino IDE serial monitor.

We have to enable telnet utility in Windows for this. Visit https://www.wikihow.com/Activate-Telnet-in-Windows-7 to know how to do this.

Simple Arduino web server

In Chapter 8, Arduino Ethernet Shield,and this one, till now, we implemented simple networking projects with Arduino. In the earlier chapters, we studied the hardware components in detail. In the remaining part of this chapter, we will combine the lessons we learned in the hardware interfacing and network programming with Arduino to create a few amazing projects.

Let's create a simple web server project where we can check the status of a device. We will use a push button, a 10k resistor, a breadboard, and a few male-to-male jumper wires for this. Build the following circuit for the demo:

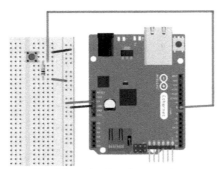

Circuit for a simple web server demo

In the preceding circuit, we're just connecting the pushbutton and resistor to the digital pin 8 or Arduino Ethernet. We are going to write a simple program to detect the keypress and change the state of the button on keypress. The following is the code:

```
#include <SPI.h>
#include <Ethernet.h>

byte mac[] = { 0x90, 0xA2, 0xDA, 0x10, 0x81, 0x42 };

IPAddress ip(192, 168, 2, 3);
EthernetServer server(80);
EthernetClient client;

void setup()
{
  Serial.begin(9600);
  if (Ethernet.begin(mac) == 0)
  {
      Serial.println("Failed to configure Ethernet using
DHCP");
    Serial.println("Assigning IP address manually");
    Ethernet.begin(mac, ip);
  }
  delay(1000);
  server.begin();
  pinMode(8, INPUT);
  Serial.print("Web Server address: ");
  Serial.println(Ethernet.localIP());
}
```

```
void loop()
{
  client = server.available();

  client.println("HTTP/1.1 200 OK");
  client.println("Content-Type: text/html");
  client.println("Connnection: close");
  client.println();

  // Code for HTML web page

  client.println("<!DOCTYPE html>");
  client.println("<html>");

  // HTML Header

  client.println("<head>");
    client.println("<title>Arduino  Webserver  Tutorial</ti-
tle>");

  // Referesh the page displayed in the browser every second
      client.println("<meta    http-equiv=\"refresh\"   con-
tent=\"1\">");

  client.println("</head>");

  // HTML Body

  client.println("<body>");
  client.println("<h1>Arduino Webserver Tutorial </h1>");
  client.print("<h2>Switch is:  </2>");

  if (digitalRead(8))
  {
    client.println("<h3>ON</h3>");
  }
  else
  {
    client.println("<h3>OFF</h3>");
  }

  client.println("</body>");
  client.println("</html>");

  delay(1);          // giving time to receive the data
```

```
    client.stop();
}
```

In the preceding program, the setup() section is similar to the earlier example where we are initializing serial and starting the server. We are also setting digital pin 8 as an input. In the loop() section, we are writing the code for a webpage that will be visible in a browser. We are using simple HTML code for this. In the same section, we are checking for button press and changing the state on the webpage. Once you upload the code to the Arduino, open the serial monitor. It will show the IP address of the Arduino web server. In my case, the address is 192.168.2.2. Open the browser on your computer and type this IP address. You will be able to see a webpage as follows:

Response from Arduino Web server

If you press and release the pushbutton, it will change the status on the webpage. We have already added the provision to refresh the page every second, so this should be instantaneous.

Arduino-based home automation

In the preceding demo, we retrieved the data from an Arduino web server to check the status of a device (in this case, a pushbutton). In this section, we will see how to send data to Arduino over the network and change the status of the devices. For the demo, we will need three 220 ohm resistors, three LEDs, and a few male-to-male jumper cables. Prepare the following circuit:

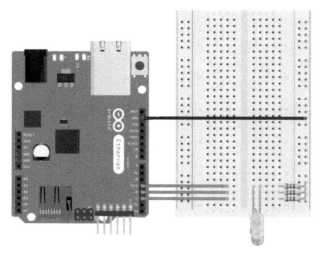

Circuit for Arduino home automation

Prepare the circuit as shown in the preceding diagram. We're just connecting digital output pins 2, 3, and 4 to LEDs through resistors. Once done, upload the following code to Arduino:

```
#include <SPI.h>
#include <Ethernet.h>

byte mac[] = { 0x90, 0xA2, 0xDA, 0x10, 0x81, 0x42 };

IPAddress ip(192, 168, 2, 3);
EthernetServer server(80);
EthernetClient client;

int led1 = 2;
int led2 = 3;
int led3 = 4;

String readString;

void setup()
{
  Serial.begin(9600);
  if (Ethernet.begin(mac) == 0)
  {
      Serial.println("Failed  to  configure  Ethernet  using
DHCP");
    Serial.println("Assigning IP address manually");
    Ethernet.begin(mac, ip);
  }
  delay(1000);
  server.begin();
  pinMode(led1, OUTPUT);
  pinMode(led2, OUTPUT);
  pinMode(led3, OUTPUT);

  Serial.print("Web Server address: ");
  Serial.println(Ethernet.localIP());
  digitalWrite(led1, LOW);
  digitalWrite(led2, LOW);
  digitalWrite(led3, LOW);

}

void loop()
{
  client = server.available();
  if (client)
```

```
if (readString.indexOf("?button3on") >0)
{
    digitalWrite(led3, HIGH);
    Serial.println("LED 3 has been turned on...");
}
if (readString.indexOf("?button3off") >0)
{
    digitalWrite(led3, LOW);
    Serial.println("LED 3 has been turned off...");
}

 //clearing string for next read
 readString="";


     }
   }
 }
}
}
```

In the preceding code, in the setup() section, we are initializing LEDs 2, 3, and 3 in the output mode and also beginning the Arduino server at port 80. In the loop() section, we are printing six hyperlinks on the webpage. When we click on any one of the links on the page, it sends a GET request to the Arduino web server. The request is succeeded by a string that is decoded by one of the six if statements in the loop() section. Depending on the string in the GET request, Arduino toggles the status of one of the LEDs. This arrangement works well as we can select only one link on the page at a time. Type Arduino's IP in the address bar and following will be the output:

Home automation project webpage

Arduino and Twitter

Let's try a more advanced yet functionally simple example. We will post to a Twitter account with Arduino. For this, we will need to install the Twitter library. Download the zip file from the link http://playground.arduino.cc/uploads/Code/Library-Twitter-1.3.zip. Once downloaded, open the Arduino IDE and in the menubar and navigate to Sketch ->Include Library ->Add .ZIP Library. Browse the location of the zip file and add the library:

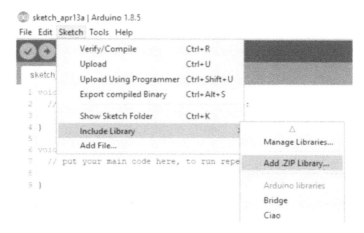

Adding a library to the Arduino IDE

Obtain your Twitter token from http://arduino-tweet.appspot.com/. To obtain the token, login with your Twitter credentials. Once you login, the webpage will show you an alphanumerical token. Copy that token to a notepad. The code to use the token and post to Twitter is as follows:

```
#include <SPI.h>
#include <Ethernet.h>
#include <Twitter.h>

byte mac[] = { 0x90, 0xA2, 0xDA, 0x10, 0x81, 0x42 };

IPAddress ip(192, 168, 2, 3);
Twitter twitter("Your-Token-Here");

// Message to post
char msg[] = "Hello, World! I'm Arduino!";

void setup()
{

  delay(1000);
  Serial.begin(9600);
  Serial.println("connecting ...");
  if (Ethernet.begin(mac) == 0)
```

```
  {
    Serial.println("Failed to configure Ethernet using DHCP");
    Serial.println("Assigning IP address manually");
    Ethernet.begin(mac, ip);
  }


  if (twitter.post(msg))
  {
    int status = twitter.wait(&Serial);
    if (status == 200)
    {
      Serial.println("OK.");
    }
    else
    {
      Serial.print("failed : code ");
      Serial.println(status);
    }
  }
  else
  {
    Serial.println("connection failed.");
  }
}

void loop()
{
}
```

In the preceding code, we're creating a Twitter handle with the authentication token that we copied from the webpage. The line Twitter twitter("Your-Token-Here") creates the handle. Replace the string in the statement with your token from the webpage. Once the handle is created, we can post a tweet with the post() function. Upload the preceding program and open your Twitter page. The result should be as follows:

Twitter Post with Arduino

Summary

In this chapter, we built a few projects by merging the hardware and networking knowledge we gained in Chapter 8, Arduino Ethernet Shield, to create simple IoT-based projects. We started the chapter with a few simple networking projects and then moved on to build IoT applications that can be used in the real life. We also saw how to post to Twitter with Arduino. In the next chapter, we will study how to setup Arduino Tian.

Exercises for this chapter

Complete the following exercise to broaden the understanding ofthe topics we learned in this book:
The earlier project that we implemented toggles the LEDs through the Web. We can extend the same circuit to toggle the status of the electrical appliances in the home. For this, I want all the readers to explore an electrical component by themselves.The component is a relay board. It does not require knowledge of a separate library. A relay is an electromechanical switch that turns a device on and off depending on the input signal provided to it. The following is an active low relay board with an array of four relays .

An active-low 4 relay board

The board has six input pins (as highlighted above in the red rectangle). There are two power pins (VCC and GND) and rests of those pins are inputs to the individual relays in the array. Each relay has three output terminals. The top two terminals are connected when the relay is active. This set of terminals is known as normally closed. The bottom two terminals are disconnected when the relay is active. This set of terminals is known as normally open. And the reverse is true when the relay is de-activated. The top two terminals are disconnected and the bottom two terminals are connected. The input to the relay should be +5V for signal. The relay output terminals can handle AC as well as DC current. They can handle up to 10A of 250 Volts of AC current with up to 60Hz alternating frequency. The relay above is active-low. It means that the relay is active and the normallyclosed part of the relay circuit connects when the input pin for that particular relay is low. The active high relay boards are also available in market. Those active-high relay boards are usually colored in green.

As I mentioned earlier, we do not need a special library to control relays. The function digitalWrite() is sufficient for working with relays.

Now we know how to work with relays, we can use them in the home automation projects. In the last projects, we just need to connect the digital output pins of Arduino to the input pins of relay board to automate our homes. Then we just need to route the electrical connections of the home appliances through the relays on the board to enable them for IOT.

NOTE: Be very careful while working with live AC voltage. An electric shock by live voltage may kill you instantly by stopping your heart function or damaging the vital organs of your body.

Chapter 10

Arduino Tian

In Chapter 9, Arduino IoT Projects, we learned how to use the Arduino Ethernet Shield to create a few exciting IoT projects. In this chapter, we will explore another model of Arduino, Arduino Tian. This chapter covers the introduction of Tian and its initial setup for the readers to get comfortable with a microcontroller packaged with a Linux-based single-board computer. In the next chapter, we will explore how to use Tian for IoT projects.

Arduino Tian

Till now, we extensively worked with Arduino Uno. In this section, we are going to get familiar with a member of Arduino family that runs Linux. And, the member is Arduino Tian. The following is the top view of Arduino Tian:

Arduino Tian top view

The pins placement is very similar to Arduino Uno. However, the names of the pins are printed on the sides:

View from a side

The following is the view from the other side:

View from the other side

There are ports for power, Ethernet connection, and USB as follows:

View from the front

Let's discuss the technical specifications of Arduino Tian.

The new Arduino Tian board has Atmel's SAMD21 microcontroller. It features a 32-bit ARM Cortex® M0+ core with clock speed of 48MHz. It has 256KB of flash memory and 32KB of SRAM.

Tian also has a Qualcomm Atheros AR9342, which is a MIPS processor operating at up to 533MHz. Qualcomm Atheros AR9342 supports a Linux distribution called Linino, which is based on OpenWRT. Arduino Tian has an in-built 4GB eMMC memory. It also has 16MB of additional flash memory. Tian features 64MB of RAM. The operating voltage of Arduino Tian is 3.3V.

Atheros AR9342 has IEEE 802.11n 2×2 2.4/5 GHz dual-band Wi-Fi module for connectivity. It also features an 802.3 10/100/1000 Mbit/s Ethernet port for connectivity to the wired networks.

Though the pinout of Tian is similar to Uno, the functionality of the pins is better than Uno. In this chapter, we will mainly focus on Linux and Atheros AR9342. So, we won't be discussing the pins in detail. However, if you are interested in the pins, then visit https://store.arduino.cc/usa/arduino-tian for more information.

Let's get started with Arduino Tian. Before we begin, we need to install the SAMD boardsfor the Arduino IDE. It's very simple. We have to use the Boards Manager in the Arduino IDE.

From Tools in the menubar, navigate to **Board ->Boards Manager:**

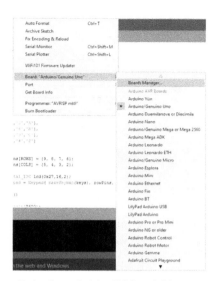

Navigating to Arduino IDE Boards Manager

Once in the Boards Manager, install the Arduino SAMD Boards (32-bits ARM Cortex-M0+):

Installing Arduino SAMD boards

Make sure that you are installing the correct set of boards by checking that Arduino Tian is in the description. Once installation is done, we need to power up the Tian board to get started. To power it up, we have to provide 5V and minimum 600mA of power using a micro USB cable. The following is a picture of a micro USB cable:

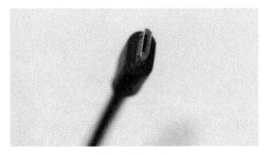

Micro USB cable

for the Tian board to boot up, load the OS, and enable the Wi-Fi access point. After around 20-30 seconds, check the Wi-Fi networks available on your computer. You will find a new Wi-Fi network named as Arduino-Tian-XXXXXXXXXXXX. The following is the screenshot of Wi-Fi networks available to my computer after I power the Tian on:

Arduino Tian's Wi-Fi

Connect to this network, and once connected, open any web browser of your choice. Type http://192.168.240.1/ in the address bar and press enter. The following page will appear:

Arduino OS login page

This is the login page of Arduino OS. Arduino OS a lightweight web-based interface on top of Linino Linux. The default password for any Tian board is arduino (all lowercase letters). Once you click on the Login button, it takes us to the **Arduino Configuration Wizard**. This wizard helps us to setup Arduino Tian for the first time (it is also available afterward through the menu; we will see that soon). The following is the first page of the wizard, the Board Settings page:

The Board Settings page

You can set the board name, timezone, and password. If you do not provide a password here, it will retain the default password. Click on Next, and the Wireless Settings page will appear:

The Wireless Settings page

You can find all the wireless networks available in your area here. Select the same Wi-Fi network to which your current computer usually connects to. We will access Arduino Tian through Wi-Fi once we are done. Enter all the relevant details such as security and password for your Wi-Fi network and click on Next. It will take you to the Rest Api Settings page as follows:

The Rest Api Settings page

Keep this at default setting and click on the Next button. It will take you to the SAVE AND RESTART page as follows:

The SAVE AND RESTART page

Click on the Save button or click on Back if you want to change something. Once you click on the Save button, a progress bar will appear as follows:

Progress bar

Once Tian is applied with new settings, it disables the built-in Wi-Fi access point named **Arduino-Tian-XXXXXXXXXXXXX** and connects to the Wi-Fi network we mentioned in the setup wizard.

Congratulations! We have setup Tian. Now, we have to access it. For this, we need to find its IP address. The easiest way to do that is to check your Arduino IDE as follows. Open the IDE and create a new blank sketch. Choose **Board: "Arduino Tian"** as follows:

Choosing Arduino Tian from Tools-> Board

You must have noticed that an entire new category of boards has been added to the IDE. This is because we installed SAMD boards before we got started with the setup process. Once done, under the same menu, that is, Tools, choose the option Port. It will look as follows:

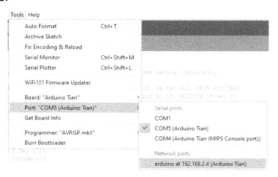

Choosing Arduino Tian from Tools-> Board

In the preceding screenshot, we can see that under **Network ports**, we can see the name of our Arduino Tian **arduino** (I have kept it at default name settings) and an IP address listed against it. Note down this IP address for now. Remember that the most of Wi-Fi networks use DHCP to allocate IP addresses dynamically. So, next time the IP address may be different.

Now, open any browser of your choice. Type this IP address in the address bar and press Enter. You will see the login screen again. However, this time, we are accessing Tian as a wireless station rather than as an access point:

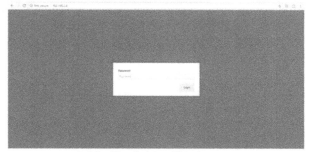

Arduino Tian Arduino OS login screen

Enter the password and click on the Login button:

Arduino OS desktop screen

This is the Arduino OS screen. You can control the Tian board in every possible way from here. Let's discuss the icons on the screen onebyone. On the right-hand side in the top-right corner, we find a set of icons:

Icons in the top right

The first option is to make the current window of the browser full screen. The second icon has the sign out and reboot options. They are visible once clicked on.

In the left-hand corner at the top, we see the Arduino logo. It is an icon for Arduino OS menu. Click on it, and it will generate a drop-down menu as follows:

Arduino menu

Let's see the menu options one by one. Under Development, we find the CodeMirror code editor as follows:

CodeMirror code editor

We can save the code files for various programming languages as shown in the following screenshot.

Under **Multimedia**, we find the **Preview** utility, and under **Office**, we have the **Calculator** application. Under **System**, we find the Settings application that is used to change the look and feel of the Arduino OS. Under **Utilities**, we have many useful applications that a developer needs on a day-to-day basis:

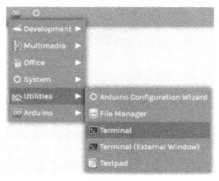

Utilities

In **Utilities,** we have the **Arduino Configuration Wizard** that we used to setup the Tian board. **File Manager** is a file explorer. **Terminal** is the command-line interface. **Textpad** is a text editor.

The most powerful is, of course, the **Terminal**. It is the commandline of Linino Linux distribution. Open the **Terminal** application. It will ask you for the username. Remember that there is only one user as of now, and it is the root user. The password that we set during the initial setup is the password for the root. Enter the password, and you will see the prompt of Linino OS as follows:

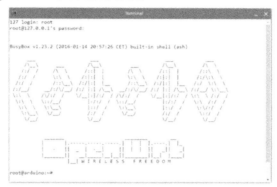

Linino Linux prompt

The prompt reads *root@arduino: ~#.* This is because root is the username. arduino is the machine name that is set during the setup process. This is the normal Linux prompt. Most of the Linux commands work without any problem. Let's see how to install and manage utilities using this.

We can use the opkg utility to manage the packages. It is the package manager like apt. Its full form is **Open PacKaGe Management.** We can use it to install a lot of useful utilities. Linino does not come with gcc, the GNU C Compiler. Install it using the following command:

opkg install gcc

Linino has Python 2. We can verify it by running the following command:

python –V

We can install the Python's package manager pip with the following command:

opkg install python-pip

We can install Python 3 with the following command:

opkg install python3

These were a few essential tools for the developers. We can exit the prompt by running the following command:

exit

We can remotely access Arduino Tian's Terminal by PuTTY or any other utilities.

Finally, we can shut down Tian by running the halt or poweroff command on the Terminal.

We find many more useful utilities under the **Arduino** option in the menu:

Arduino menu

Of these all utilities, Arduino System Log and Arduino Kernel Log are log-viewing utilities for more experienced developers. Arduino Process Viewer is a utility to view and manage currently running processes. The following is the screenshot:

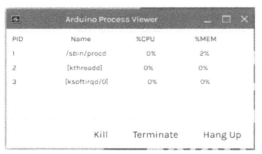

Arduino Process Viewer

Arduino Package Manager is graphical version of the opkg utility. It is used to install new packages and manage already installed packages. The following is the screenshot:

Arduino Settings application window shows us the information about the Tian board:

Arduino Package Manager

Arduino Settings

Arduino Luci is a control panel-type application. Once you click on it, it asks you the root password:

Arduino Luci login

Once you enter the password and click on the Login button, you will be taken to the application. Using this application, you can accomplish many things. Explore it more on your own. The following is the screenshot:

Arduino Luci monitoring option

This is the brief overview of the Arduino OS and Linux. Now, let's see how we can use Arduino IDE to upload the programs to Arduino Tian. Shutdown the microprocessor of Arduino Tian using the halt command. Once done, open the Arduino IDE on your computer and open the Blink sketch from Examples in the File menu. Make sure that you have chosen the Arduino Tian option under Board in the Tools menu. After that, open the Ports option from Tools. The following is the screenshot:

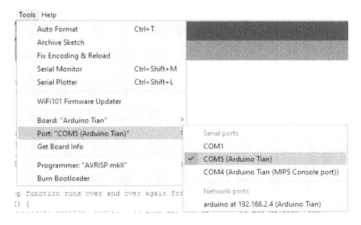

Arduino Tian over serial and network ports

We can upload program using the COM serial port when Arduino Tian is connected to the computer using the USB cable. While choosing the port, choose COM5 (Arduino Tian). Here, in my computer, Tian is connected using COM5 and COM4. In your case, it could be different ports. Do not select the COM port that reads MIPS Console Port. This option is very useful when the Wi-Fi network is not available.

We can upload program using network port when Tian is connected to Wi-Fi. This option is very useful when Tian is not directly connected to the computer using a USB cable.

In my case, Tian is connected to my computer with a USB cable, and it is also connected to the Wi-Fi. So, I can choose any of the options to upload the sketch.

You might be wondering what to do with the existing network settings when you change the Wi-Fi network. For this, there is a remedy. There is a small push button near the USB host port. It is for Wi-Fi reset. When you are in some other network and want to access this, simply push this button for 5 seconds when Arduino is powered on. This will reset the Wi-Fi settings and initiate Arduino Tian into Wi-Fi Access Point mode while retaining all other settings. We will be able to see the Wi-Fi access point corresponding to your Tian in your computer. From here, we can connect to Arduino Tian to configure it again to connect to the new Wi-Fi point.

With this, we are concluding this section and the chapter.

Summary

In this chapter, we have been introduced to Arduino Tian. We learned the specifications of Tian. Also, we had an overview of Arduino OS for Tian and the Terminal command prompt of the Linino Linux on Tian. In the next chapter, we will try to have a look at how to use Arduino to create interesting IoT projects with online IoT platforms.

Exercises for this chapter

• Try running a few Python 3 programs on Arduino Tian.
• Build and deploy all the projects that we did in the earlier chapters on Arduino Tian

Chapter 11

Temperature Sensor and IoT

In Chapter 10, Arduino Tian, we learned how to set up and get started with Arduino Tian, a Linux-based member from the Arduino family.

In this chapter, we will study temperature sensors and how to interface them with Arduino to build an IoT-based system. So let's get started with the basics of the digital humidity and temperature (DHT) sensor.

The DHT sensor

The DHT series of sensors is used for measuring humidity and temperature. These sensors have a capacitive humidity sensor, thermistor, and analog-to-digital converter. These sensors output the digital signals corresponding to the humidity and temperature values of the environment. They are easy to be interfaced with the microcontroller chips such as Arduino. The following is the list of the DHT sensors and their alternative names:

- **DHT11:** Also known by name RHT01
- **DHT21:** Also known as RHT02, AM2301, and HM2301
- **DHT22:** Also known as RHT03 and AM2302
- **DHT33:** Also known as RHT04 and AM2303
- **DHT44:** Also known as RHT05

All these sensors have four pins, and the names of these pins from left to right are as follows:

- **Pin 1 – VCC:** To be connected to +5 V
- **Pin 2 – OUT:** Output signal to be connected to the digital input
- **Pin 3 – NC:** Not connected
- **Pin 4 – GND:** Ground pin to be connected to GND

Let's get started with practically connecting the circuit and programming. The following is the circuit diagram:

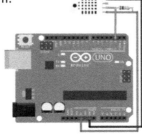

DHT22 connected to an Uno board

I am using a DHT22 (or an AM2302) type of sensor and 10 K resistor for this. DHT22 works in 1-100% humidity range and −40 to 125ºC temperature range. Its sampling rate is one reading every 2 seconds. The resistor works as a pull-up resistor for the digital I/O pin of Arduino to which we're connecting the output pin of the sensor. The connection scheme is same for all the other sensors in the family. So, if you have got any other sensor, do not worry and just connect it as shown in the preceding diagram. This was the hardware part. Let's get the needed libraries. Install the Adafruit Unified Sensor library from **Manage Libraries** in **Sketch** from the menubar:

Installing the Arduino Unified Sensor Library

Now, let's manually download and install the Adafruit DHT library. The Arduino Unified Sensor library is the pre-requisite for this library. That's why we installed it. To download the Adafruit DHT library, visit its GitHub page located at https://github.com/adafruit/DHT-sensor-library. Download the library as a ZIP file. Name of the zip file is DHT-sensor-library-master.zip. Extract the contents of the ZIP file to the current directory. It will create an output directory named as DHT-sensor-library-master. Rename this directory to DHT. Then, copy this directory to the libraries directory of the Arduino installation directory. In my computer, the location is C:\Program Files (x86)\Arduino\libraries.

If you have installed the Arduino IDE in the default directory path mentioned in the setup wizard during the installation, then the location for the libraries directory is same for your computer too. If not, then search for the directory where you installed Arduino IDE and locate the libraries directory.

Once copied, the installation for using the temperature sensor is complete. The following is an example program for using DHT22:

```
#include "DHT.h"
#define DHTPIN 2
//#define DHTTYPE DHT11   // DHT 11
#define DHTTYPE DHT22   // DHT 22  (AM2302),
AM2321 //#define DHTTYPE DHT21   // DHT 21 (AM2301) DHT
dht(DHTPIN, DHTTYPE);
void setup()
{
```

```
    Serial.begin(9600);
    Serial.println("DHT22 test!");

    dht.begin();
}

void loop()
{
  delay(2000);

    float h = dht.readHumidity();
    float t = dht.readTemperature();

    if (isnan(h) || isnan(t))
    {
        Serial.println("Failed to read from DHT sensor!");
        return;
    }
    Serial.print("Humidity: ");
    Serial.print(h);
    Serial.print(" %\t");
    Serial.print("Temperature: ");
    Serial.print(t);
    Serial.println();
}
```

The preceding program is a very simple example to read the temperature and humidi- ty from the sensor and to display it on the serial monitor. Upload the program and check the serial monitor for the output. As shown in the circuit layout, we are using digital I/O pin 2, and we have programmed accordingly. The if condition in the program checks whether the output of the sensor is valid value. The remainder of the code is pretty straightforward. The following is the output:

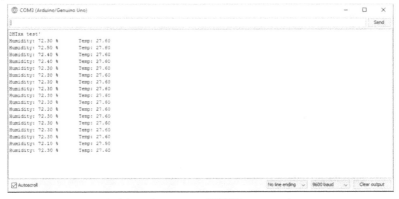

Serial monitor output of DHT22 sensor code

Arduino and ThingSpeak

Till now, we have worked on creating IoT prototypes where every component is owned and managed by us. Now, we are going to see how we can work with a third-party online IoT platform. There are many platforms available on the Internet for collecting and visualizing data from IoT-enabled sensors. We will see an online data collection and visualization platform – ThingSpeak.

ThingSpeak is a very easy-to-configure and convenient-to-use platform for IoT-enabled data gathering devices. Let's get started with this by installing the ThingSpeak library to the Arduino IDE. Just open the Library Manager from menu and type Thing-Speak in the search bar. There will only be one entry in the results. Select the library and install it. Refer the following screenshot:

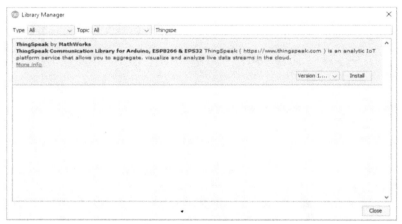

Installation of the ThingSpeak library

Once the library is installed, the next step is to create an account on the https://thingspeak.com/ website. Once you create the account, you need to create a channel. Log in to your ThingSpeak account and check the Channels option in the top-right corner. It is a drop-down menu and has a My Channels option. Select it as shown in the following screenshot:

My Channels

Create a new channel and enter the required information in the form as follows:

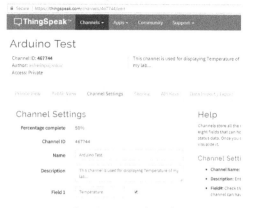

Creating a new channel

At this stage, the newly created channel is private. Go to the Sharing option and make the channel public. Refer to the following screenshot:

Making the channel public

Remember that only the owner of the channel can edit the channel settings. Making the channel public only makes the data shared on the channel available to public for viewing. Now, it is time to write some code. Before that, go to the **API Keys** option and copy your unique **Write API Key**:

Write API Key

I have masked the key with a black box because, using this key, one can programmatically write the data to my channel. If you feel that the key has been compromised, you can always generate a new key.

We have seen how to read and display environment-related data with DHT22 in the previous section. We need to use the same circuit for this example too. However, the Arduino Uno board by itself cannot send data to the Internet, so we either need to use Arduino Ethernet Shield or Arduino Ethernet board with the sensor. Prepare the circuit and upload the following code to the board:

```
#include <SPI.h>
#include <Ethernet.h>
#include "ThingSpeak.h"
#include "DHT.h"
byte mac[] = { 0x90, 0xA2, 0xDA, 0x10, 0x81, 0x42 };
IPAddress ip(192, 168, 2, 3);
EthernetClient client;
unsigned long myChannelNumber = 467744;
const char * myWriteAPIKey = "XXXXXXXXXXXXXXXX";
#define DHTPIN 2
//#define DHTTYPE DHT11    // DHT 11
#define DHTTYPE DHT22    // DHT 22  (AM2302), AM2321
//#define DHTTYPE DHT21    // DHT 21 (AM2301)
DHT dht(DHTPIN, DHTTYPE);
void setup()
{
  Serial.begin(9600);
  if (Ethernet.begin(mac) == 0)
  {
       Serial.println("Failed to configure Ethernet using DHCP");
     Serial.println("Assigning IP address manually");
     Ethernet.begin(mac, ip);
  }
  delay(1000);
  ThingSpeak.begin(client);
  dht.begin();
   Serial.println("DHT and ThingSpeak initiated successfully!");
  }
void loop()
{
  delay(2000);
  float h = dht.readHumidity();
  float t = dht.readTemperature();
  if (isnan(h) || isnan(t))
  {
    Serial.println("Failed to read from DHT sensor!");
    return;
```

```
}
Serial.print("Humidity: ");
Serial.print(h);
Serial.print(" %\t");
Serial.print("Temperature: ");
Serial.print(t);
Serial.println();
   ThingSpeak.writeField(myChannelNumber,  1,  t,  myWriteA-
PIKey);
   delay(20000); // ThingSpeak will only accept updates every
15 seconds.
}
```

Most of the preceding code is familiar to us. So, I will just explain the part we are not familiar with. In the beginning, we are including ThingSpeak.h in the program to get access to the API. In the setup() section, ThingSpeak.begin() is used to initialize the ThingSpeak API. We are storing the channel number of our channel in a variable. We are also storing the 16-character write API key in a character string. Finally, in the loop() section, we are using the ThingSpeak.write() function to write the data to the channel. For the function call, the first argument is the channel number; the second argument is the field number; the third argument is the variable; and the fourth argument is the API Key. Upload this code to the Arduino and visit the web page corresponding to your channel. For my channel, the URL is https://thing-speak.com/channels/467744. It looks as follows:

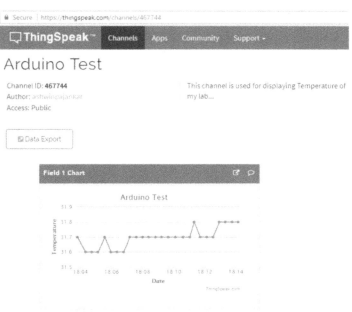

My channel displaying the temperature of my lab

Summary

In this chapter, we have created a few IoT applications with Arduino and online platform ThingSpeak. In the next chapter, we will have a look at a new IoT platform Bolt IoT.

Exercises for this chapter

In Chapter 10, Arduino Tian, we studied Arduino Tian. We learned how to use Thing-Speak with Arduino and Ethernet Shield. As an exercise you can try the Arduino Ciao library with Tian to send data to ThingSpeak. You can install the Ciao library from the Library Manager as follows:

Installing the Arduino Ciao library

In Chapter 9, Arduino IoT Projects, we saw how to post a tweet with the Twitter library. We can extend the same project to create a tweeting Arduino weather station by adding a DHT sensor to that and tweeting the temperature and humidity at a fixed interval.

Chapter 12

Introduction to Bolt IoT

In Chapter 11, Temperature Sensor and IoT, we interfaced Arduino with the temperature sensor DHT22 and sent the data to an online analytics platform ThingSpeak. And, if you have finished the exercise, then you must now be comfortable with Arduino Tian and Ciao library too.

In this chapter, we will get introduced to a recently launched IoT platform, Bolt IoT. We will get introduced to the members of Bolt IoT plarform and then learn how to set up a Bolt Wi-Fi module.

The Bolt platform

Inventrom Private Limited, a Bangalore-based start-up organization, has created Bolt IoT. Bolt IoT is, as its name suggests, an IoT platform for the developers. We can find the homepage of Bolt IoT at https://www.boltiot.com. We can also visit the crowd-funding pages for the project, https://www.kickstarter.com/projects/boltiot/bolt and https://www.indiegogo.com/projects/fully-integrated-iot-platform-made-for-ml#/. We will get started with the Wi-Fi module of the Bolt IoT platform. The following is a top-down photograph of the Wi-Fi module clearly showing the microcontroller unit:

Bolt IoT Wi-Fi module MCU and GPIO pins

The following photograph shows the other side, exposing the micro-USB port for power connectivity.

Bolt IoT Wi-Fi module micro-USB port

Let's have a look at the specifications of the Wi-Fi module. You can also find the specifications in https://cloud.boltiot.com/docs. The Wi-Fi module has an ESP8266 module for connectivity. The MCU which is at the heart of the module is Tensilica Xtensa LX106, which is 32-bit RISC CPU, and it runs at 80 MHz. It has 64 KB of instruction RAM and 96 KB of data RAM. It also has 4 MB of external flash memory. Let's have look at the pin diagram of the Wi-Fi module.

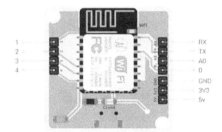

Bolt IoT Wi-Fi module pin diagram

We can power this module either through power pins 5 V and GND or through the micro-USB port. 5 V 1 A is more than sufficient for the module to operate. There are five digital I/O pins numbered from 0 to 4. They operate at 3V3 voltage. They can also be used for software PWM. We can use pin A0 for analog input. It has an internal 10-bit **ADC (analog to digital converter)** connected to it.

It can connect to a Wi-Fi AP and also server as **AP (access point)** when not connected to any Wi-Fi. It also has UART through TX, RX, and GND pins, which operate at 9,600 baud rate.

Armed with this information, let's see how we can get started with Bolt IoT. For getting started with Bolt IoT, we first need to register with their website. Sign up at https://cloud.boltiot.com/login. Once you are registered, you need to use your mobile phone to download the Bolt App.

Android   iOS

Bolt IoT App QR codes for Android and iOS

We can also check for keyword Bolt in the stores in Android or iOS for the app. Once you install the app, log into it using the credential you created earlier on the Bolt Cloud. There will be an option for adding a Bolt device to this app. Tap that option. Then, connect the Bolt Wi-Fi module you have to a 5 V power source using a micro-USB cable. Your Bolt Wi-Fi module will act as a Wi-Fi AP. You will now be prompted to enter the SSID and password of the Wi-Fi connection you have at your place. Enter those credentials. When the Bolt restarts next time, it will act as the Wi-Fi receiver and will connect to the Wi-Fi connection. Once done, you can go to the web portal where we had registered and see your device there:

Bolt IoT Cloud platform showing the linked device

Summary

In this chapter, we introduced the Bolt IoT Wi-Fi module and saw how to set it up. This was a very crisp chapter intended to get the user familiar with the Bolt platform and ecosystem. In the next chapter, we will have a look at a few IoT projects we can implement with this platform. We will also have a look at another member of the Bolt platform, Boltduino.

Exercises for this chapter

As an exercise for this chapter, readers can explore the Bolt IoT homepage and cloud portal. It will be really helpful in understanding the projects in the next chapter.

Chapter 13

Bolt IoT Projects

In Chapter 12, Introduction to Bolt IoT, we got introduced to the Bolt Cloud and the Bolt IOT Wi-Fi module. We learned how to get started with the Bolt Wi-Fi module by setting it up. In this chapter, we will explore the platform further by creating a few simple projects built around the Wi-Fi module. We will also see how to interface it with Arduino. In the end, we will get introduced to a new member of the Bolt ecosystem, the Boltduino.

Getting started

I hope that you have explored the Bolt Cloud as a part of exercise in the Chapter 12, Introduction to Bolt IoT. If not, there is no need to worry. We will explore the essentials of it and see how to use it to implement simple IoT projects with Bolt.

To get started, first connect your Bolt Wi-Fi module to a power supply. Then, log in to the Bolt Cloud portal. Once you login, in the Devices page, you will be able to see your device. You will also see that the status of the device is **ONLINE:**

Bolt IoT Cloud platform showing an online Wi-Fi module

Here, you can see the list of all the devices associated with your account. Let's go to the Products page. It will look as follows:

Building your own product

Click on the **BUILD** button. It will then bring up a screen for building a new product:

Building your own IoT product

Here, you can change the icon for your product, assign it a name, and set the properties of the Bolt Wi-Fi module. You can connect the input or output device to the module. You can collect the data over **GPIO** or **UART**. Once you finish it by clicking on **DONE**, you will see that the product is added to the product list as follows:

Building your own product

We also find a toolbar on the top-right corner of the page under the username. The first icon is **Configure**. The second icon is **Edit Product**, and it takes us to a screen similar to build a product. The third icon is **Link Device**. And, the fourth icon is **Delete Product.** Click on the Configure icon and you will be redirected to a page:

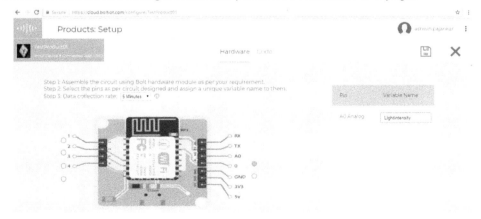

Configuring the product

In the preceding screenshot, select the radio button corresponding to the A0 pin. Also, assign it a variable name of your choice. Then, save changes to your product. Prepare the following circuit with a photodiode (also known as LDR) and a 330 ohm resistor:

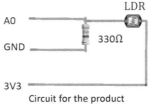

Circuit for the product

Connect the preceding circuit to the I/O and power pins of the Wi-Fi module according to the labels on the left-hand side. Once connections are made, go to the code window and choose .js as the filename. Also, set a filename in the textbox. Once done, type the following code in the code editor:

```
setChartLibrary('google-chart');
 setChartTitle('LDR Demo');
 setChartType('lineGraph');
 setAxisName('Time','Light Intensity');
 plotChart('time_stamp','LightIntensity');
```

The entire page would like as follows:

Code for the product

The second argument in the last function call in the code is the variable name that we set for the pin A0 input. Make sure that you replace it with correct variable name. Once done, just save the code and exit using icons in the top-right corner. Go to the product page and click on Link Device icon. The following screen will appear:

Link the product

Once the product is linked to the device, the following entry will appear on the product page:

Link the product

There are four icons on the right-hand side of the entry corresponding to our product. The first icon is View Device, the second icon is Unlink Device, the third icon is Share, and the fourth icon is Deploy. Click on the Deploy icon. This will deploy the code to the device. Wait for a few minutes for the product to collect the data, and then, click on the View Device icon. You should be able to see a graph similar to the following one:

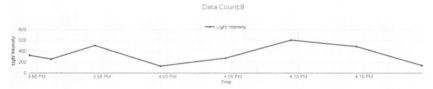

Light intensity demo

Connecting an output device to the Bolt Wi-Fi module

In the preceding demo, we connected the Bolt Wi-Fi module to an LDR and a resistor to act as an input device. In this demo, we will connect a simple LED to the digital pin 0 of the Wi-Fi module. Connect the anode pin of the LED to digital pin 0 and cathode of the LED to the GND pin of the Wi-Fi module. In the Bolt Cloud portal, add a new product and configure it as an output device:

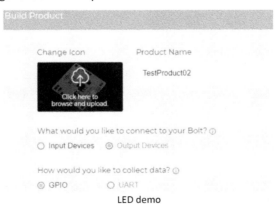

LED demo

On the product configuration screen, select the radio button corresponding to the digital pin 0 and also set a variable name. Refer to the following screenshot:

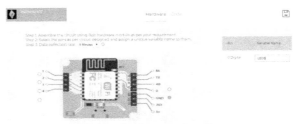

LED demo hardware configuration

Paste the following code in the code editor and save it as an HTML file:

```html
<html>
<head>
  <!-- In following line will load the boltCommands.js files
from Bolt cloud.-->
    <script  type="text/javascript"  src="https://cloud.bolt-
iot.com/static/js/boltCommands.js">
  </script>
 <script type="text/javascript">
    // The following line will set the API key and device
name. It will be auto-initialized by Bolt cloud.
    setKey('{{ApiKey}}','{{Name}}');
</script>
</head>
<body>
<center>
  <!-- In below line, we are calling the digitalWrite function
from  boltCommands.js file to switch on the LED. -->
    <button onclick="digitalWrite(0, 'HIGH');">ON</button>
  <!-- In below line, we are calling the digitalWrite function
from boltCommands.js file to switch off the LED. -->
    <button onclick="digitalWrite(0, 'LOW');">OFF</button>
</center>
</body>
</html>
```

Save the code by clicking on the **Save** icon. If you have noticed, the code requires the API key and device name. Exit the screen and go to the **API** page in the Bolt Cloud portal. Generate an API key:

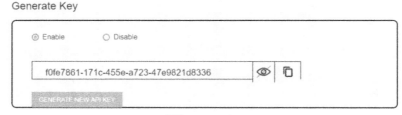

API key generation

Copy this key and your device ID and insert them in the preceding code in the line where the setKey() function is called. It should look similar to the following line of code after adding the API key and device ID:

setKey('f0fe7861-171c-455e-a723-47e9821d8336','BOLT3431947');

The API key will be unique for every user and device combination, and if you feel that your key has been compromised, you can always generate a fresh key.

Once you make changes to the code, save the code, and link the device and deploy the application. After deployment, when you click on the **View Device** icon in the product listing page, it will take you to the following web page:

The web page for controlling the LED

Enjoy toggling the status of the LED by clicking on the buttons.

Interfacing the Bolt Wi-Fi module with an Arduino board

We can interface the Bolt IoT module with an Arduino board. Connect the Tx pin of the Arduino board to the Rx pin of the Bolt IoT Wi-Fi module and connect the Rx pin of Arduino board to the Tx pin of the Bolt IoT Wi-Fi module. After that, connect the GND pins of both to each other and do the same for the 5V pin. Once done, go to https://github.com/Inventrom/boltiot-arduino-helper and download the ZIP of the Bolt IoT Arduino Helper library. Then, open the Arduino IDE, and in the menubar, navigate to **Sketch -> Include Library -> Add .ZIP Library**. Browse the location of the .zip file and add the library:

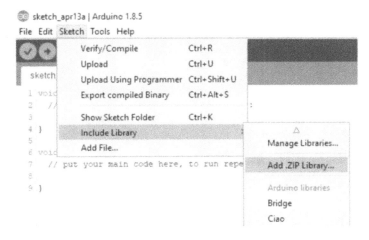

Adding a library to the Arduino IDE

Once the library is added, write the following code in the IDE, save, and compile it:

```
#include <BoltIot-Arduino-Helper.h>

void setup()
{
  boltiot.Begin(Serial);
  pinMode(2,INPUT);
}

void loop()
{
  boltiot.CheckPoll(digitalRead(2));
}
```

In the preceding code, we are reading the digital input from digital pin 2 of the Arduino board and then sending it to the Bolt IoT over serial bus. We can configure a new product in the Bolt IoT Cloud where the communication mode is UART.

 Disconnect Arduino from Bolt while uploading the code.

Boltduino

Bolt IoT has come up with an Arduino clone with a provision to directly mount the Bolt IoT Wi-Fi module. The following is a photograph of Boltduino board:

Boltduino board

There are 11 header pins on the right hand side (near the micro-USB interface) in the photo above. We can use them to directly mount the Bolt IoT Wi-Fi module as follows:

Bolt IoT Wi-Fi module mounted on the Boltduino board

We can simply program the Boltduino board as another Arduino Uno board by selecting Arduino/Genuino Uno from the Arduino IDE. To facilitate the interfacing with the Wi-Fi module, we can use Bolt IoT Arduino Helper library we saw in the preceding section.

Summary

In this chapter, we started creating a few simple projects with the Bolt IoT Wi-Fi module. We also saw how to interface the Bolt IoT module with the Arduino board. Finally, we saw the Boltduino board, a clone of Arduino Uno. In the next chapter, we will have just a brief overview of a few members of Arduino family, which are used for IoT.

Exercises for this chapter

Download the project book for Bolt IoT from https://www.boltiot.com/project-book.html and implement the projects from it.

Chapter 14

Wrapping It Up

In Chapter 13, Bolt IoT Projects, we saw a couple of simple projects with Bolt. We saw how to interface the Bolt Wi-Fi module with an Arduino board. We also saw a new member of the Bolt family, Boltduino. In this short chapter, I will introduce you to a few members of the Arduino ecosystem, which can be used for IoT conveniently. We won't be learning coding these Arduino boards as that comes under the scope of another separate book. However, I will mention the reference websites where readers can find more information about the libraries.

Arduino Yún Rev 2

In Chapter 2, Introduction to the Arduino Platform, there is the mention of Arduino Yún. Arduino has recently released a revised version of Yún and named it as Yún Rev 2. As of writing of this book, its specifications are not available on the Products page at https://store.arduino.cc/usa/arduino-yun-rev-2. It is estimated to be available in April 2018. The following is a photo of it:

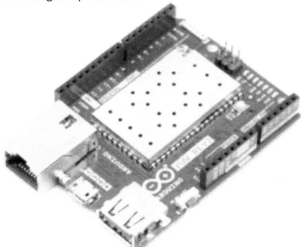

Arduino Yún Rev 2

You can read about the announcement of Arduino Yún Rev 2 on https://blog.arduino.cc/2018/03/29/arduino-yun-rev-2-is-here/. You can find a few projects at https://create.arduino.cc/projecthub/products/arduino-yun-rev-2. We can also use the Bridge library for all the Yún devices. Documentation and sample projects for the

Bridge library can be found at https://www.arduino.cc/en/Reference/YunBridgeLi-brary.

Other Yún devices

Other Yún devices are Industrial 101, which is the original Yún with a different form factor.
Yún Mini is compact version of the original Arduino Yún.

Arduino Yún Mini

Another prominent member is Yun shield. It can be mounted on any Arduino Uno board to make it function like Yún. You can find more information about it at https://www.arduino.cc/en/Guide/ArduinoYunShield. Its clone is Draguino Yún Shield. You can find more details at http://www.dragino.com/products/yun-shield/item/86-yun-shield.html. As I mentioned earlier, all the devices in Yún family can use the Bridge library.

Arduino GSM shields

Arduino GSM shields are used to connect Arduino to cellular networks. There are two revisions of this. Revision 1 is not in production anymore, but available for purchase. You can find more information about it on https://www.arduino.cc/en/Main.Ardu-inoGSMShieldV1. The latest revision, revision 2, is in production, and you can find out more about it at https://store.arduino.cc/usa/arduino-gsm-shield-2-integrat-ed-antenna.

Summary

In this short chapter, we had a very brief look at a few IoT-enabled members of the Arduino ecosystem.

Conclusion

We started our journey of IoT with learning the concepts of IoT. Then, we got introduced to the Arduino ecosystem and interfacing the Arduino board with various hardware components. Equipped with basics, we moved on to connecting Arduino to the Internet. Once we understood how to connect Arduino to the Internet, we combined that with hardware interfacing and created a few amazing IoT projects. We also explored the setup and basics of Arduino Tian. Finally, we saw a brand new IoT platform Bolt IoT and implemented a few projects with it. I hope that the readers enjoyed reading this book and following the examples as much as I enjoyed writing the book and creating all the prototypes. However, the journey does not end here. This is just the beginning of an era where IoT will be pervasive. IoT is like an endless ocean that hosts many pearls and hidden treasures. It is really worth to explore it.